PURSUIT

One man's quest to find God's perfect will for his life.

Ken McDonald B.D., Th.M.

FIRST EDITION

ISBN 978-0-9798844-0-5

Personal Photo by Dirk Travis, Sierra Photography, Sonora, CA

For additional copies, please contact:
Evangelist Ken McDonald
1107 S 5th Ave., PMB 118
Yuma, AZ 85364

www.kenmcdonaldfamily.com

Printed in the United States by
Morris Publishing
3212 East Highway 30
Kearney, NE 68847
1-800-650-7888

Thank You

I would like to thank those who have helped on this book. Especially Wanda Stein, and Danilee Varner for their excellent proof reading.

To my daughter Rebekah, thank you for your excellent work designing and creating the cover.

Thank you Daryl Heimbold and Helmut Ghetto for your encouragement to write this book.

Dedication

This book is dedicated to my dear wife, Terri, who has gone through many trials because of my lack of discernment, and confusion as to the perfect will of God. Yet, she has remained faithful and true to the Lord Jesus Christ first of all, and then also to me.

Prov. 31:25 Strength and honour are her clothing; and she shall rejoice in time to come.

Table of Contents

Introduction ix

1 The Call to Preach 1

2 Bible School 21

3 First Trip Out 55

4 Back to Pensacola 73

5 Back to California 81

6 Twain Harte 93

7 Montana 129

8 Valley Springs 143

9 Washington 155

10 The Bottom 173

11 Back on Our Feet 191

12 Jubilee Baptist Church 201

13 God's Will, Finally! 207

14 God's Help 215

INTRODUCTION

What you are about to read is an account of what I went through, and what I took my family through, in order to find God's will for my life. It has not been an easy book to write for it is a very transparent record of the mistakes that I made over the years trying to find God's will. As I reflect on the many mistakes, they now appear so "stupid," yet, I made them over and over, due to my not seeing what the Lord was evidently trying to show me.

Like a child learning to walk, I tripped and stumbled on for many years in search of the Lord's will for my life. I would not recommend finding God's will the way I did, for I made many foolish and hurtful mistakes. But in spite of the mistakes, I did finally find God's will for my life, and that will is like a treasure of inestimable worth. There is no amount of gold or silver that could be as valuable as finding, and then doing the will of God for your life.

Pursuit

God's will varies from person to person. I do not know what the Lord's will for your life is, and no one can tell you what it is. You must find it yourself as the Lord deals with you. Others may give you advice, and they may be right, but you must decide it for yourself between you and the Lord Jesus Christ.

One thing that I do know is that God's will for you, according to His word, is that you be born again. The Bible says that, *The Lord...is longsuffering to us-ward, not willing that any should perish, but that all should come to repentance.* (2 Pet. 3:9) *Ye must be born again.* (John 3:7)

If you have not been born again, then you are out of God's will right now, and there is no way you will ever do God's will for your life until you first ask Jesus Christ to forgive you of your sins, to come into your heart, and save you from Hell. There is no one else who can save you, and there is no other way to Heaven.

John 14:6 *Jesus saith unto him, I am the way, the truth, and the life: no man cometh unto the Father, but by me.* This is the very beginning of your quest to find God's will for your life. If you do not start here, you will never spiritually proceed any further, since the quest to find God's will is a spiritual one.

Will you ever hear the Lord say to you, *"Well done, thou good and faithful servant?"* (Matt. 25:21) The only way you will ever have the joy of hearing the King of the Universe, the Lord Jesus Christ, say those words to you is to find God's will for your life and do it. Though your attempts to find His will may cause many tears to fall, (bankruptcy, loneliness, and the like) yet to find His will is worth it in this life, and far greater in the life to come.

My one piece of advice to you who are attempting to

find His will is this, "DON'T QUIT!"

CHAPTER 1

THE CALL TO PREACH

As I stepped out of the old, faded, tan, four-door hatchback, I felt the arid, yet refreshing breeze blow across my face. It was dusk and the constant noise of cars and trucks speeding by filled the air, though a high sound barrier fence separated us from interstate 10, the eight lane freeway that was just on the other side of the barrier.

Don, a tall, largely built, easy going man, slowly got out of the driver's side of his car. I had met him six months earlier when I was saved, and he had been discipling me since then. Many hours, patiently, he had taught me Bible, and we prayed together on our knees.

We both looked around with pleasant amazement at the many people who were getting out of their cars also. It was Central Baptist Church, and a Wednesday evening service. The white building was very large, rectangular and about four stories high, with a roof that almost looked oriental in architecture as it curved outward at the bottom and was smaller at the top. Small rectangular windows were scattered throughout the walls of the building, each one a different colored glass. It was a very unique building, and nothing like I had ever seen before, especially for a church building.

What had brought us this evening to Central Baptist Church, besides the Lord, was the fact that we were looking for a good church to attend while we worked as traveling salesmen. We were working Southern California. The previous Sunday we had attended a service at a Presbyterian church that we had heard of, but the services were rather dull, to say the least. We left in search of another place to attend.

Don had been receiving a Christian newspaper called, "The Sword of the Lord." It is a fundamental Christian newspaper with printed sermons and other articles in it. It also had advertisements of churches from various parts of the world, but mainly the United States. As I was looking it over I saw an advertisement for Central Baptist Church in Pomona, California. Being that we were about thirty minutes away, we decided to give it a try.

I felt a bit intimidated as I entered the large building. There were many other people entering also. Some of them were dressed for church, and some were still in work clothes. But with Bibles in hand, we entered, not knowing what to expect. We were just two strangers who had dropped by for the service.

The auditorium was very large and could seat about two thousand people. We walked down the aisle and sat in the center section, a little over half way back on some hard, unpadded brown wooden pews, and waited for the service to begin.

As I sat there, I thought of the little Baptist church back home in the foothills of California. I had only been saved six months, and with no religious background all I knew was the little church back home. It was a liberal church, compared to this one, but still the church back home was more formal and stiff.

Little did I know that this night my life would change. Little did I know that by the end of the service I would never again be the same. It was the Spring of 1978, maybe May, and though I don't remember the exact date, I never will forget the night.

By the time the services started there were about 700 people in the auditorium. The choir of about 50 people were seated in the choir loft behind the pulpit. The choir director came out, addressed them, they all stood and started to sing. They opened with the hymn, 'Wonderful Grace of Jesus,' and what I noticed immediately was that their hearts seemed to be in it as they sang with genuine joy on their faces. It wasn't just a show. This was something I had never seen before.

Then the pastor, a tall, dark-haired, fair complected man, in his late forties or early fifties, dressed in suit and tie, entered the pulpit and began to preach- I mean really preach. He was raising his voice, sweat ran off his brow down his cheeks, and it was obvious he meant what he said. He clenched his fist, pounded the pulpit and preached from the text in John 9:4 *I must work the works of him that sent me, while it is day: the night cometh, when no man can work.*

He preached about the work that needed to be done for the Lord, and that there was coming a night when it would be too late to work. The night of communism, the night of old age, the night of death, the night of tribulation were four of the points that I remember. My mind did not wander; my attention was riveted to this preacher and his sermon as he compassionately and fervently preached.

Though there were other points I don't remember, that night, as the preacher preached, there was a fire that began to burn in my heart. It was a fire of purpose, a purpose to live. Until I was saved, life had no reason to be lived. Salvation had given me a hope and something to look forward to. I knew I was going to Heaven when I died. But that evening the Lord reached over heaven and touched me in a way that changed me again, as much, or more, than the change that took place when I was saved.

As Pastor Batema ended his sermon, he gave an invitation to come forward to the prayer altar and get things right with the Lord. I had never heard of the term, "called to preach." All I knew was that I had to go forward.

I stepped to my left and Don moved back so I could get out. Down the long aisle I walked with tears beginning to stream down my cheeks. Nobody knew me there that night. I was eighteen years old, had been saved about six months, knelt at the altar, and started to cry.

A personal worker knelt beside me and asked if I was saved, and I said, "Yes." He then asked what I came forward for, and I told him that I wanted to preach. With that I completely broke and wept at the altar. After five or ten minutes, I filled out a form with my name and address and decision. I gave it to the worker and stood at the front row.

Each card was read by Pastor Batema from the pulpit, which was about five feet higher than the floor where I stood. When he came to my name he said, "Ken McDonald." I tried to look up, but was still crying. He looked at me and read the decision, "Called to preach." I tried to speak but couldn't, and then he said, "It looks like the Lord is still dealing with him." I could only shake my head yes.

Six months earlier, when I had been saved, my life greatly changed. But that night it was changed again. I would never be the same again until the day I died. I had been called to preach.

Many people came and shook my hand. I just looked out through blurry, tear-filled eyes. I remember Don coming up and holding out his hand to shake mine. He said, "Congratulations Ken." All I could say was, "Thank you."

We left the church that evening, got back into that faded tan car and started for the motel. But I was not the same person that I was before we arrived. Thoughts of our home church and it's spiritual deadness intersected with the reality of the condition of so many people back home who were not saved and on their way to Hell. Spiritual and eternal things were now more real to me, coupled with the call to preach, I couldn't keep my mouth shut. I started "preaching" to Don.

From that night to this, I have always known that I was, "Called to preach." That night, the Lord Jesus Christ called me to preach the word of God.

If I had to describe the call I don't know if I could adequately do it. But ever since that Wednesday night service, there has been something that moves me, something inside my soul that was not there before.

It's not a living thing that entered me, like when the Lord entered my body when I got saved, but more of a burden on my heart. It's a yearning to proclaim the word of God in churches, on streets, or anywhere there are people. I can't help but think of preaching anytime there are people around.

The call to preach consumes me at times. There is not a day that goes by that I don't think of a sermon to write, of how to preach a little better, or of when the next time I preach will be.

It keeps me awake at nights thinking of preaching to large crowds and people getting saved. And it is a pressure, a burden that I can never get away from. It goes where I go.

As you will read, in my years of searching for the perfect will of God for my life, there were times the pressure and burden of the call became very frustrating to have. The effort that I had put out to fulfill the call kept ending up in failure, yet the call remained there to drive me on.

I heard a story one time about a famous preacher, who I believe was Vance Havner, though I am not sure. In a nursing home, bedridden and weak, he had lived a life of faithful service, preaching the word of God and winning many to the Lord Jesus Christ.

One day some young preachers came by to see him. They walked into his room, and there in the bed lay a man whom God had used. A preacher, whose sun was about to set, was now ready to cross over Jordan and go home to Heaven. He was so weak he did not move his body, only his lips moved, but being so weak, the young preachers could not hear what he was saying.

One of the young men bent over and put his ear close to the old preachers lips. In an almost whispered voice, the words that were coming from those lips that had proclaimed the word of God for so many years were, "I must preach, I must preach."

The body was worn and weak, yet the burning call to preach that God had placed there so many years earlier, still pushed the old preacher on to proclaim, "I must preach."

The Lord of Glory, Jesus Christ, had now placed that call in me. From here on I was, and am, in a pursuit of God's will for my life.

It was the Spring of 1978, I was eighteen years old, and for the first time in my life I had a reason to live. I was saved around November 29, 1977. I'm not sure of the exact date. Just a kid from a little town up in the Sierra Nevada mountains of central California called, Twain Harte.

Both of my parents were college educated, and though they did the best they knew how, there was no religion of any kind in the home. They divorced when I was in high school. The emptiness that was there from being raised without God was now growing into a disillusionment and a search for a reason to live.

Money, things, and popularity were all things that I searched for, and to a certain extent attained. But my soul was empty, and no amount of booze or drugs could fill the void.

When I was saved in November that emptiness was filled by the only thing, or should I write, the only person who could ever fill it, the Lord Jesus Christ. I no longer needed the booze and the dope. Peace flooded my soul, and life took on a whole new meaning.

Now, with the call to preach, there was purpose, a reason to live. A worthwhile reason that I had never had before. I began to understand in a very real way that the reason I was alive was to serve the Lord Jesus Christ. To do His will. As Paul had, I prayed, *"Lord what wilt thou have me to do? Yes, I know that you want me to preach, but what next? Where do I go from here? What is your perfect will for my life?"*

The quest to find the answer to that last question would be a quest that would take me seventeen years to discover. It would take me thousands of miles, cost me thousands of dollars, and have me shed many tears. There would be suffering and hardship like I had never known before.

It would all be for the purpose of finding out, and then attempting to fulfill, the whole reason why I am alive; to do God's perfect will for my life.

I have never gotten over the fact of what a privilege it is to serve the King of the universe, who also is my Creator. Not only is it a privilege, but it is also my duty as one of His creatures, or creations, to serve Him.

This privilege is not deserved as I am no good. The Bible says that *there is none good, but one, that is, God.* (Matt. 19:17) If I got what I deserve I would be in Hell right now. Aside from that, before I got saved there was no reason to live. Life was empty and had no meaning. I was like a leaf that falls from a tree growing over a stream. The leaf lands in a whirl pool and spins around going nowhere.

He not only gave me eternal life when I was born again, but He also gave me a more abundant life now. A life with purpose and meaning. But that life would be wasted if I did not pursue His will for my life.

To me God's will is a treasure of inestimable worth. There is nothing more valuable than His will, His desire for me. As Jesus prayed to the Father, *"Not my will, but thine be done."* (Lk. 22:42) His will is like the air I breathe or the water I drink. Without the doing of His will, there is no life, or reason for me to live.

If I am a created being, and I am, then my Creator ought to have supreme say so in my life. After all, if He created me and gave me life, then He could just as easily take my life, if He so chose to.

Does this mean I serve Him out of abject fear? Not at all! It is just an acknowledgment of who I am in relation to who the Lord Jesus Christ is as the Creator of the universe, and the Creator of me. Rev. 4:11 *Thou art worthy, O Lord, to receive glory and honour and power: for thou hast created all things, and for thy pleasure they are and were created.*

Then, the only way my life will ever be fulfilling and satisfying is to live the way I was created to live, and serve Him the way I was meant to serve Him. Otherwise if I live for me, then life becomes a bleak void full of confusion, mixed with sparse moments of pleasure, and futile attempts to sustain happiness and fulfillment.

When you live the way you were designed to live, life becomes internally peaceful. When you live for yourself apart from God's will for your life, then your life may be externally peaceful, or it may not be, but either way, internally you are miserable.

The pursuit of God's will started in me at the point of salvation, but then that pursuit intensified when I was called to preach that night at Central Baptist Church in Pamona.

When I was called to preach the Lord did some things to me. Ever since the call to preach, it has been difficult to keep my mouth shut. I had to, and have to talk, about the Bible or the Lord. It's something that was put in me that night. I've noticed that when preachers quit preaching and have to get a job, generally they get a job that they have to use their mouth, such as selling cars or insurance.

That night, Don and I left Central Baptist Church. He said practically nothing because I was the one doing all the talking. As we headed back to the motel, Don drove as I preached in the passenger seat.

Amongst the thousands of rushing cars and trucks that night on the Los Angeles freeways was a little tan four door with a man and an eighteen year old teenager preaching to him all the way back to the motel.

"Why don't the people in our church back home care about the lost going to Hell? The preacher never raises his voice. He never preaches on salvation, Hell or Judgement? Why, it's nothing but a social club where they are playing church, and there are souls all around going to Hell!" I would wipe the tears out of my eyes and keep on preaching to Don. He didn't mind. He had discipled me, and I can't help but think the Lord allowed him to be there that night to see me get called to preach.

A month or two later we were back home, and the church, though nervous about this rapidly growing youth group, had a youth service. It was a Sunday evening service where the youth did it all: song leading, piano playing, announcements, and preaching.

I don't remember how we were chosen, but Russ Hoover and I were the ones chosen to preach that evening. Russ had been instrumental in me getting saved, and with Don, he also helped me greatly grow in the Lord.

I studied much, which was not something I used to do. I prayed and prayed, and studied some more in order to be ready to preach that evening. My notes were typed out and just about memorized.

The service started fine, and Russ was chosen to

be the first one to preach. Keep in mind that this is a semi-formal church, and when an hour is up, the service is over and everybody clears out in ten minutes or less.

Russ began preaching and he had a real good sermon. He was preaching out of Isaiah 40. But as time went on I began to get a little worried. There wasn't going to be time for me to preach.

The service started at 6:30P.M., and at 7:20P.M. Russ apologetically looked down at me and shrugged. By the time he was finished it was 7:30P.M., and time to go.

No way! I prepared this sermon, and I've got to preach. The fire that burned in me, the urgency in my soul, all culminated in me standing up and going to the pulpit to preach. I think, if I remember correctly, that as I stood up I said, *"We're not done yet."* What could they do? They had to stay overtime. This was the youth service, and the youth were going to do things a little differently.

I preached for a half hour on the subject of hinderances to prayer, finishing at about 8:00P.M. We all laughed about it later. There were a few sour looks on some of the faces, but, for the most part, they didn't mind the extra time.

You know, it's funny, the things you see when you look back. As they say hindsight is 20/20. When I was finished preaching that evening, one of the girls in our youth group came up to me and said, "You reminded me of Frank Gonzales." He was an evangelist that had come to the church for a revival.

I see it now, but at the time I did not see it. I reminded her of an evangelist, not a pastor or missionary, but an evangelist. You may think it to be just a coincidence, but that is not the case, as there would be more such instances in the future.

When she said it to me I was shocked, and then thought nothing of it, until later, years later. I suppose that was the first sign that God was going to use me in the field of evangelism. But did I see that at the time? Not at all!

As I look back, another thing that seemed to point me into the field of evangelism was my job. When I got saved I was working at a grocery store, and in the store they sold liquor. Little by little I became more uneasy about selling liquor, and four or five months after my salvation I quit and started working for Don as a traveling salesman.

This was a whole new adventure for me. A traveling salesman working strictly on commission. The product that we sold was haircombs. Sounds strange doesn't it? You may have seen, usually in quick stop stores, plastic round tubs of combs. That is what we were selling. There were many things about it that are similar to the way I live in evangelism.

For one, you are on the road all of the time, living out of a suitcase, eating in restaurants, and meeting new people. Often times you are low on money (well, I was because I was not a good salesman.) Don or Russ would literally double or triple the amount of sales I had. But cars would break down, and you would have to fight staying awake at the wheel when you would drive.

That first year of my salvation was such a life changing year, and yet it seemed like God's will was much easier to find. I suppose it was because my Heavenly Father would take me by the hand and lead me in the way I should go. He was teaching me to walk by faith and not by sight. The joy was how He would hold my hand and lead me in those days when I was just a new babe in the Lord.

After I was saved, I went to church or a Bible study every night for a solid thirty days. The next month, I went to church or a Bible study every other night. Then these Bible studies began to grow in number of people coming. We also began to realize that there are some very big differences in the Bible versions. By the time Don and I visited Central Baptist Church we had just come to the realization that the old King James Version of 1611 was and is, the inerrant word of God.

It was after I learned that the King James Bible was the inerrant word of God, that He called me to preach. And He called me to preach in a church, and through a preacher that believed that the book he read from and preached from was the Holy Bible without error.

This is very important because when a man, not a woman, but a man, is called to preach, he is called to preach the word of God. If you don't have the word of God then you can't preach it.

This is not to say that God doesn't call men to preach from churches that don't believe they have the inerrant word of God, I'm sure he has. But with me, He waited until I knew where the word of God was, and that I could hold it in my hands, and preach from it proclaiming *"thus saith the Lord"*, instead of my own worthless opinion.

Realizing that the King James Bible is the word of God, coupled with the call to preach, combined with a young man who had a zeal for God, but not according to knowledge, and you have all the making for...trouble. Not malicious trouble, nor was I trying to cause trouble. As a matter of fact, I was trying to do right, and please my Lord. It's just that the other more "dignified and seasoned" members of the church didn't see it that way.

The spiritual condition of my home church troubled me. Partly because my family was lost and I wanted them to get saved. There was this thought I had, that if my church would get "on fire" for the Lord, maybe my family would get saved.

One day before the morning service I arrived at church early and stuffed Chick tracks in all of the pews. (They are small pamphlets on various spiritual subjects.) I put them where the visitor cards went. I stuffed them with the tract, "Why No Revival" but, I ran out of those, so I used what I had left which was, "The Last Generation."

If you don't know, the first one was about the sins of the average church, and most of the sins mentioned were common in our church. The second tract was about the mark of the beast and the antichrist, which was strong meat for that church. They knew who was behind it, and the people who desired the status quo didn't like it.

During this time in my life I was praying about where to go to school to study for the ministry. I had made a few more trips down to the Los Angeles area, and on one of them Don and I took a trip over to San Demas to check out Pacific Coast Baptist Bible College.

It was in a beautiful setting at the foot of a mountain. It also had a nice campus. We looked around and found our way into the bookstore. I looked at a few books they had. But what was on my mind was whether they believed the King James Bible was the word of God without error?

I kept looking around and then I found some yearbooks from the previous years at the school. As I thumbed through them, my heart raced with anxiety as to whether or not this was where the Lord wanted me to go to school. I turned a page in the yearbook and saw what convinced me that it was not His will for me to go to school there.

I was looking at a picture of about 15 students in a circle who were holding hands with their heads bowed in prayer. That is not bad, don't get me wrong. But under the picture it read, "There's a sweet, sweet spirit in this place," taken from the charismatic song. One look and I knew that was not the place for me. Along with the social club, and the don't offend anyone, be positive attitude at First Baptist Church, there was also a huggy, hand holding, charismatic influence that I wanted no part of.

There was only one place left that I knew was a place that believed the King James Bible was the word of God, and that place was Pensacola Bible Institute.

Central Baptist Church had Dr. Ruckman's books in their bookstore, and it was through those books that I decided I would go there to school.

I began to make preparations the spring of 1979, when I sent them my entire tax return to pay for my first semester of school.

Things at church and home continued to go bad.

I was living at Grandma T's, (T stands for Tessie.) Though she was not a blood relative, she was as close to me as my own mother. Tessie was concerned about me ever since I got saved.

One night, about 11:00 P.M., I really "freaked her out." (A little California lingo there.) I had been to revival services, and the preacher had preached on Rock music. He mentioned about different groups that ask Satan to bless their albums and to send a devil out with each album. This really spoke to my heart. The Lord dealt with me that night to get rid of all of my Rock-N-Roll records. These days you would call them "Vinyl." I didn't want any devils in my house.

That night I came in the house about 11:00 P.M., and Tessie was getting ready to migrate to the bedroom and settle down for the night.

In the living room was a large old fashioned stone fireplace that could hold at least three thirty-six inch logs at one time. The living room was all knotty pine, and the steep vaulted ceiling was two and a half stories high to the apex.

As I walked into the living room, I was a young man on a mission. I had one thing on my mind, and that was to get rid of my record albums. I was going to burn them right then and there.

The fire had almost died out when I arrived, so I went out and got some more wood to put on the fire. Tessie saw what I was doing and said that, I didn't need to do that, as we were going to bed.

I tried not to say much knowing that she would not understand anyway, but there was a strong determination in my heart. So I just said in a low muffled, but determined voice, *"No, I need to do this."*

With a concerned reply she quickly asked, "Do what?" I gave her no reply. I thought to myself, *"She will see soon enough."*

After putting the wood on the fire, I then went over to my fairly large collection of Rock-N-Roll albums, and started picking some of them up.

Tessie, now more concerned, stuttered and fearfully asked, *"Wh, wh, what are you doing?"*

I threw a few into the fire and they started to burn,

still giving no reply knowing that it would be useless to try to reason with her.

I then replied to her, *"I'm burning my albums."* While saying this I did not look at her, nor did I stop what I was doing. I was focused on my task at hand, and no one was going to stop me.

Tessie stood up, and said, *"Oh Kenny, you're getting too fanatical!"*

I believe I replied rather indignant, *"Do you want me to go back to my dope, is that what you want?"* I just kept throwing more and more records into the fire.

Most of the lights were out in the living room, the glow of yellow flames danced and reflected on the knotty wood grained walls. Looking across the dining room, and into the living room where I was, Grandma "T" shook her head with tears in her eyes. All she could say was, *"Oh, Kenny, you're going too far."*

I didn't care; I knew I was on the right road for the first time in my life, and, by the grace of God, I was determined to stay on that road.

That road now included Bible school, and the school was 2500 miles away. Needless to say, I was a bit intimidated at the thought of going that far. Of course, the Lord was, and is with me, but, I had no pastor or church supporting me. I had no family supporting me. What I was going to do for the Lord was going to be done on my own.

The Lord knows what we need in times like this to nudge us along. Deut. 32:11 *As an eagle stirreth up her nest, fluttereth over her young, spreadeth abroad her wings, taketh them, beareth them on her wings.* The Lord was stirring up my nest and getting me ready to fly.

Tessie had gone on a senior citizen excursion to

Reno, Nevada. It was a trip to go gambling in the casinos. On that trip was a man from my church. She laughed about it, and kind of threw it back in my face, as though it was a big joke boasting to me, "I guess V_____ M______ is going to Hell because he went gambling with us." I did not take it that way.

Here I was trying to lead my loved ones to the Lord, and people from my own church are stumbling blocks to them getting saved.

With some anger welling up in me, I prayed and looked in the word of God. It said, *"Wherefore, rebuke them sharply, that they may be sound in the faith."* (Titus 1:13) Okay, then I will go talk to the deacons board at the next deacons' meeting. Being called to preach, my "talk" was a bit more than a talk.

This was the beginning of the end for me in the church. But I went into the deacons' meeting that day. I had my points all lined up and ready to go. Underneath my calm demeanor was a simmering fire.

They were all there. The deacons, and the deaconesses. Even though the Bible says a deacon must be the husband of one wife, yet they had deaconesses. One of the "lady deaconesses" even taught the adult Sunday School class, though the word of God says, "Suffer not a woman to teach." (1 Tim. 2:12)

I waited and waited until all of the reports from the various committees were read. Finally, the head deacon hesitantly asked, is there any new business? I said yes, that I had some business that I would like to bring up.

They said to go ahead, and I did. I was nervous and my heart was pounding as I looked at the board of deacons. Along with the nervousness was a certain amount of anger and frustration with the church. All of this emotion combined with the call to preach, and it spelled trouble.

With my notes prepared, and in hand, I proceeded to tell them my complaint. I preached to them that women shouldn't teach the men and read the verse to them. A lady ran crying out of the room. I then mentioned that we ought to use the King James Bible as our final authority in all matters of faith and practice. Well, that would do away with the deaconesses, See Romans 16:1 in any other version, and then in a King James.

Other ladies began to cry, and then the men started to get upset. I asked, *"Why don't we have sermons on gambling, hell, Judgement, and the blood?"* It basically was the same sermon I preached to Don on the way to the motel the night I got called to preach.

Here is a church that is doing little to nothing to try to win the souls in those hills to the Lord Jesus Christ. That thought broke me, and I began to cry.

There was much discussion for a while and finally the meeting ended.

A week or so later, the assistant pastor, who also worked with my own mother at a local elementary school, came up to me after church. He was a very personable kind of man that everyone liked. He put his hand on my shoulder and said, *"Ken, you know one of the things the Lord hates is someone who sows discord among brethren."*

So here it was. Here was my answer. In so many words he was telling me that if I didn't quit my trouble making that I would have to leave the church. If I didn't like it here then maybe I needed to move on.

I replied, *"Rick, I'll be leaving for school soon. It won't be long, I will be gone."*

There was a comfort in my soul that day. It was a confirmation to me, that it was God's will for me to leave and go to school.

Ah Yes! God's will. That aspiration that now gave me purpose, and a reason to live.

Chapter 2

BIBLE SCHOOL

It was the middle of August, 1979. A time of year that is associated with hot sultry days and nights known as the "dog days" of summer. But up in those California mountains, it is not that way. At least not around the little mountain town called Twain Harte, where I had lived the first eighteen years of my life.

It is a small town of under a thousand people, nestled in the Sierra Nevada mountains at about 3800 feet elevation. The mountain air is scented from the tall sugar pine, incense cedar, black oak, and ponderosa pine trees. It is a place that has four distinct seasons and all of them are beautiful. Also, because of its small size, you always saw people you knew. Whether driving to town or walking the road, there was always someone to wave to. It had that sense of belonging that only comes from being a part of a small close community, and even more so for me since I had lived there all my life.

In the summer, many people came up there to vacation and rest from the hustle and bustle of the cities, like San Francisco, Oakland, and even people from the Los Angeles area came up there. Some of the visitors were famous movie stars, like Michael Landon, who had a cabin up there. George C. Scott's ex wife, who was a star in Ben Hurr, lived just down the road from me.

I looked around at the house I had grown up in. It was a nice house of middle class status. My mother and father were both college educated people who worked for the California school system. They divorced when I was in high school, and after that, life became one big party until the day I was saved, which to the best of my recollection, was on November 29, 1977.

But this little town and area had been my home. We had never moved around. I grew up right here, and now I was leaving.

There was a mixed emotion in my soul. Part of me was saying, let's get out of here. God wants me at Bible school, glory to God, let's go! And there was another side that enjoyed those mountains. The cool breezes, as they blew through the tops of the pines, would play a melody that would soothe the soul like no other, for it was a melody produced by God himself. It was a place where you felt like you were always on vacation.

Those mountains have a way of working into your heart, and you will never get them out of there as long as you live. If it wasn't for God's will, I probably would never ever leave those mountains until death. I've always been glad when I think of Heaven and realize that it is a mountain, *Beautiful for situation, the joy of the whole earth, is mount Zion, on the sides of the north, the city of the great King.* Psalm 48:2

It didn't take long to load up my old faded blue 1966 VW Bug. I didn't have that many things left to take with me. When I got saved I read in the Bible where it said, *"Sell that ye have,"* and I did just that.

Before I was saved, money and things were a big part of my life. I started working when I was eleven years old. I would mow lawns and do yard work. Then, I went to work at the local grocery store. With the money that I had coming in, I would save up and buy whatever I wanted.

By the time I was seventeen I had all kinds of things, such as guns, fishing equipment, ski equipment, 35mm camera, nice guitar, fancy stereo, etc. I had all kinds of junk.

When I got saved all of that stuff didn't mean much to me. I sold a lot of it real cheap, and gave money away to the work of the Lord. I realized that those things didn't make me happy, it was Jesus Christ that made me happy.

The things I loaded into the old VW were my guitar, some Christian study books, my Bible, some clothes (including two suits), and the product that I sold as a traveling salesman.

I got in the car with excitement racing through my soul as I realized that I now had purpose. I was leaving to go to Bible school. The Creator of the universe had a job for me to do, and I was taking my first step in the pursuit of that job.

I do not know what it feels like to be a millionaire, but a millionaire could never feel more rich than I did that day, or as I do this day. Not only was I saved and going to Heaven, but I also had the most valuable possession any human could have on this earth, and that is, a call from the Lord Jesus Christ to serve Him. Me, an aimless worthless sinner from the hills of California, and I was going to study the Bible and prepare for a life of service for the King of Kings!

When I was lost, I grew up believing that I had evolved from an ape. I believed that evolution was true. But the older I became the more I would think and wonder, "Ken, what are you going to do with your life?" And I could never find an answer to that question.

There was no reason to do anything. Why would I want to make money? As a younger teenager I liked making money, but now it was losing its appeal. Why should I go to college? To get a better job? Why get a better job? In order to make money to buy things that can't provide happiness? Nuts!

I would ask people these questions, but there was no satisfactory answer given to me. Usually the answer was, "Because that is what you are supposed to do. After all, you don't want to be poor, do you?" These thoughts taunted me day after day, and night after night.

But inside I was poor, I was empty. So to me life became a bleak void of darkness that no one could give me light to see through. Until I got saved. Then I realized that Jesus Christ is the answer to all of my searching. I am to live for him and no other. I am so rich! I felt so grateful to the Lord for showing me why I am alive.

As I started the old VW these thoughts raced through my mind with a joy that made me want to shout. I get to serve the King of the universe; I am so rich!

I pulled out of Twain Harte the middle of August, 1979, less than two years after getting saved. Nobody saw me off. There were no hugs. No one was there to say, "I will miss you." There was nobody there to see me off, except my Savior. He was there, as well as the angels.

My Savior, the Lord Jesus Christ was looking over the bountiments of Heaven with a smile on His face. He said to me that He would never leave me nor forsake me, and that He would always be with me.

There was no headline in the local newspaper, or on the six o'clock news. But in Heaven they all saw me off, and to me that's all that mattered. The praise of man pales when compared to the smile of God.

I drove down to Los Angeles and met Don where we worked for a couple of days. In those days I had no pastor that I could go to for advice. That may have been good, or it may have been bad, I don't know. But, I had no other man to look to for any spiritual guidance other than Don. What he said to me carried a lot of weight.

Because of this, (and I am not putting the blame on anyone but myself for this) I failed to do God's will in a certain matter that I will now describe.

A couple of months before my leaving for school, I met a man back home in Twain Harte. He had just been saved, as a matter of fact, I think he got saved there in Twain Harte. But he had just come from the casinos of Las Vegas. His name was Bill Eubanks, and he was excited about the Lord.

When I met him I had a copy of Dr. Ruckman's commentary on Exodus in my hand, and he asked if he could borrow it to read, so I lent it to him. He thoroughly enjoyed it and returned it to me. When he did, I told him that I was leaving soon for Pensacola Bible institute where Dr. Ruckman taught.

He said that he would like to go to school also, and

asked if I would be willing to give him a ride to school. I said that I would.

There was just one thing that he had to take care of before he left, and since I would be leaving from Los Angeles, would I be willing to pick him up in San Diego. I said yes, and the plan was set. Bill left for San Diego a few days before I left for Los Angeles.

With Bill already gone, and counting on me to pick him up, Don found out about our plan. I know Don meant well since he had nothing against Bill at all, but he was worrying about me.

Don told me that I would be going way out of my way to pick up Bro. Eubanks. *"You know Ken"* he started, *"If God wants you to go to school, the devil is going to sidetrack you any way he can. I don't think it is God's will for you to give him a ride to school."*

When I heard that this might be a trap to keep me from doing God's will, fear gripped my heart. I've got to do God's will, and maybe this is a trap. I hardly know this man. Don says I ought not to go out of my way, but head straight for school. If Don says it, then that is what I will do.

It's a hard thing to know when to listen, and when to ignore advice. But, in this instance I listened and called Bill up and told him that I would not be coming to get him. I broke my word, and let down a brother in the Lord. So many times I have regretted this decision. I am thankful that Bill ended up at school in spite of me, though he arrived a semester later. In time I had to apologize to Bill; I had let him down, and I had not kept my word.

It was now heading into the third week of August, 1979 and time to leave Los Angeles and head off to Bible School. With $60.00 in my pocket, my few possessions, and an adequate amount of product to sell, I began my two thousand mile trip to Pensacola, Florida.

Don and I hugged, knelt and prayed. Then I was off to Pensacola Bible Institute. Heading East on interstate 40 I was just outside of Needles, Arizona, on the California Arizona line, in triple digit temperatures. My VW bug had no air conditioner, but I was used to it-well, kind of.

All of a sudden, I felt a rear tire start thumping, bumping, and then, the tread separating. The tires were retreads I had bought a few months earlier, but they had good tread on them. The tread had peeled off one of them but, praise the Lord, the tire was still holding air and had not gone flat.

After stopping and looking at the tire, for I had no spare, I got back in and limped slowly into Needles, Arizona.

Stopping at one of the first gas stations I found, I asked if they had a tire I could buy. The man went into the shop and, yes, they had one for $55.00 with mounting. I had $60.00 and about three quarters of a tank of gas.

I told the man, *"I'll take it,"* and he installed it on my car. I now had $5.00, three-quarters of a tank of gas, some combs, and 1800 miles to go to make it to Bible school.

I worked the rest of the day, which I believe must have been Friday. With a few sales, I was able to get a motel room and a bite to eat.

Saturday I worked my way east, but sales were very slow. By the end of the day I had a choice, put the little money I had in gas, or get a motel. It was Saturday night, and Sundays are not known to be days for selling things, but my "Ox was in the ditch" Luke 14:5, and I had to get him out. After prayer, I decided to get a motel, which left me with around two dollars.

Sunday morning I started working the area. Breakfast took the rest of my money, and I was working and praying. Driving into a campground, I found the camp store, and praise the Lord, I made a sale. By the end of the day, I had enough money to go farther east.

All along my journey, I would make a sale here and there. With my heart thrilled and excited to think that I was going to Bible school to learn the Bible to learn to preach it was as if I was floating on joy all the time.

I was cutting southeast, through Texas when I looked in my rearview mirror and saw red lights flashing. It was a small town, and the main road I was on went right through the center of town.

My car was not registered and the plates were old and out of date. I had tried to get it registered in California but the hippie I bought the car from never gave me the right papers, and I had been driving on temporary registrations for six months. By the time I left, the temporary registrations had run out, but I still did not have the proper papers in order to get the car registered in my name.

The afternoon sun beat down on my little car, as I sat there, an eighteen year old boy far from home. I waited for the officer to walk up to my window. I kept my hands on the steering wheel, and of course, all of my windows were rolled down. In a slow, southern Texas drawl he said, *"Ah clocked ya doin 47 in ah 45 mile per hur zone."*

There in an old faded blue VW bug that could have

easily gone for a hippie bug, I looked up at the officer and said, *"I'm sorry officer, I didn't realize I was going over the speed limit."*

He asked for my driver's license, and then walked back to his car to run the plates. I prayed and said, *"Lord help."* My thoughts raced in my head thinking he is going to find out that this car is not registered, and then what will I do?

A few minutes later he slowly walked up to my car again with me still sitting there. *"Yah car aint registered." "No sir,"* I replied *"I have tried but have not been able to get the papers needed."* Sweat continued to run down my back as well as my face.

The officer looked through my back window checking me out. *"Where yah headed?"*

When he asked that question my face lit up with joy. The thought of going to Bible school thrilled me, and with a big smile on my face, and a joy that filled my voice, I brightly said to him, *"I'm headed to Pensacola, Florida to go to Bible school."*

He paused for a moment with a slight astonishment not expecting my reply, looked again into my back window and probably saw my Bible. He then said, *"Well, when yah geet thar you'd better have that taken care of,"* and handed me my drivers license back.

"Yes sir, officer, I plan to" was my reply, and on south eastward I traveled.

Later that day, I was stopped at a stop sign with fields of high corn stalks all around, when I looked up into my rearview mirror I saw that a '65 Ford Mustang was coming up on me fast, and there was no way he was going to stop in time. Before I could do anything he swerved and went over to the dirt farming road that ran along side the road.

Waving as he slid by, he got the car under control and went back onto the road continuing on to wherever he was going. I, with a sense of supernatural protection, smiled and said, *"Thank you, Lord, for watching out for me."* And then, I went on down the road.

It was late in the evening when I arrived in Houston, Texas. I was tired and looking for a Motel 6, my home away from home. Driving down the boulevard to the motel I noticed the sidewalks were polkadot-ed. I'd never seen something like that before. I thought to myself, *"That is strange that they would have polkadot sidewalks."* I arrived at the motel and got out of the VW Bug. I looked down, and it wasn't polkadots, it was bugs! Big bugs! I later came to know them as Palmetto bugs, or roaches. They were the type of bug that when you stepped on them your foot would slide a little as the bug was squashed beneath your shoe. I had never been that far east in the USA, and things were sure different.

About a week after leaving California, I arrived in Pensacola, Florida. Don had a sister who lived there with her husband, and they had agreed to put me up for a while. I found their house, met them and unpacked my things in the spare bedroom they graciously offered to me.

The very next day, I don't know what day it was other than it was a day in the middle of the week, I drove over to the school. Finally, I made it.

With my first semester already paid for, I walked into the bookstore office which was on the same grounds as the church and the school, and which also was the only thing open. The lady at the desk was intently reading an article. She looked up at me, and with a big smile I said, *"Hi!."* She slowly cautiously replied,

"Hi." Then with eager excitement I said, *"I'm here to go to Bible school."* She replied, *"Huh?"* I replied, *"I'm here to go to Bible school, and I have my first semester all paid for."*

She calmly looked over to another man, Danny Clipper, and said, *"I think you need to show this young man around the school."* And so I went on the tour of the "plush" facilities of the Pensacola Bible Institute, which consisted of one stucko building containing four rooms. Two smaller class rooms, a small break room, and a larger auditorium room. That's all it was.

To the world it didn't look like much, but to me it was a palace. It was where I was going to learn the Bible, and how to preach and serve the Lord Jesus Christ. It was where I was going to prepare to do the only thing in my life ever worth living for and that was to serve the Lord Jesus Christ. My Lord had called me to preach, He had led me here to learn how, and my oh my, was I ever excited!

Three days after my arrival in Pensacola, hurricane Frederick hit and gave me a welcoming party. Things were not going well with Don's sister and her husband so I started looking for another place to live.

At school I heard about a man that was looking for a roommate. I was introduced to him and asked if he wanted a roommate, and he said that he did. We agreed on the plan, and I moved into the small house that he was renting.

I had never been east of the Mississippi. So many things were different. John Hooker, the man whom I was now renting from, was a southerner and about ten years older than me. He was from Arkansas and had been a tank driver in the army.

John and I are still friends. He is a good man and

with his wife, Leslie, is serving the Lord to this day. At the time though, he was single.

I remember those first weeks of school so well. Most of the time I would sit at my desk and stare at Bro. McGaughy, the assistant pastor at the time, and a teacher in the school. I couldn't believe I was in Bible school, and there was a certain fear Bro. McGaughy instilled in me after the first time I heard him preach.

But, I would come home from work and study for Greek. Since I was attending school at night, I would get home before John and study my Greek conjugations, dipthongs, and vocabulary. John would come home after a day of laying carpet, and get in the shower and start to sing. In the living room, with these horrible, off-key, made up songs, echoing through the house, I would plug my ears and try to continue in my memorization.

Another thing I was not used to was John's Arkansas accent. He would say to me, *"Ah'm goin' ta bol sum ahggs."*

Confused, I would ask, *"What?"*

He would repeat, *"Ah'm goin ta bol sum ahggs."*

Still confused, *"I don't know what you said."*

He would say it a little more deliberately, *"I'm goin' to b..b..b..boil sum ahggs."*

"Oh," I would reply, *"You're going to boil some eggs."*

We had quite a time, John and I.

The old run down house was quite a place too. Roaches roamed freely throughout the walls, as well as Palmetto bugs. One night as I knelt in prayer in the dark before I went to bed, I heard a flutter in the room. I kept praying, and one of those big roaches flew right up my pajama leg. I didn't scream, but I moved fast and smashed the creature right on my leg. Another night I had one fly and hit me in the mouth, thank the Lord my mouth was closed. I've heard of fried roaches to eat, which is bad enough, but raw and alive is really bad. Such was my introduction into the South.

Upon arrival at school, and with Don's urging by phone, I tried to continue to be a traveling salesman, but more and more I did not have peace about it. Don continued to "sell" me on the idea, and I continued to travel during the day, and go to school at night.

Sales were down, and so was money. My old VW was broke down and not running. On a Saturday, when John was home, I asked him if I could borrow his car to go out and work.

My lack of steady employment, and lack of money was beginning to bother John, as well as myself. He let me take his car, and I put what little product I had to sell in the back seat of his army surplus AMC four door Ambassador and headed off to work.

I never will forget the day. I had been praying about quitting the sales job, but I wasn't sure if it was God's will or not. Don kept pushing me to keep selling, but I didn't have peace about it. I prayed that if I could just sell the rest of my stuff I would quit the sales.

For the first half of the day I had zero sales. Not even a close one, and I was getting discouraged, as well as pressured, for I needed some money. Then about 2:30 in the afternoon I made a sale. The next store I went in I made another sale. Then the next store, and the next, and by 4:00 P.M. I was sold out.

As the sales were picking up I sensed that John was praying for me. When I got home I told him that I had sold out, and had the money I needed. I then asked him, *"Were you praying for me?"* He said the Lord spoke to his heart about 2:30 P.M. and said, *"If you want Ken to sell those things you had better pray."* And so he did. Every store bought until I was sold out because John had prayed for me.

The Lord showed me that day that it was time to quit the traveling salesman job, and get something else. He had been showing me for some time, but I do have a problem with listening to what others say instead of doing what I believe God wants me to do.

The Lord had sent me to Pensacola to go to school, and He didn't want me traveling all around the country, He wanted me in Pensacola. I ended up getting a job at a grocery store.

I worked at the grocery store during the day, and went to Bible school at night until 10:00P.M. Night after night I had the privilege to sit and get fed the word of God. I had many questions answered about life and eternity.

Month after month the Bible was being infused into my heart and mind, and little by little I was getting spiritually charged up more and more.

Along with this, was my call to preach which made it hard to keep my mouth shut. I knew it was possible, but I just couldn't keep my mouth shut.

At the little southern grocery store I would talk to the boss's son about Bible and related topics. He was rather worldly and liked to argue. I would get into heated discussions with him often, and the boss would come by and say, *"Get back to work!"*

Then in the Spring, long about March or April, I started slipping gospel tracts into the grocery bags when I would bag the groceries. I did this for about two weeks.

One of the store's best customers complained about getting gospel tracts in the grocery bags. By the time they complained to the boss, Mr. Stringfield, I had stopped slipping tracts into the bags. Mr. Stringfield was an older man getting ready to retire, and to sell the store. He had that slow Southern talk, and was fairly easy going. Yet he was the owner, and my boss.

One morning as we were getting ready to open the store, I was back in the meat department. Mr. Stringfield came back there and was getting some meat ready to put out. He then asked me pointedly, "Have you been putting pamphlets in the grocery bags?"

I replied, "Yes..." and was about to say that I wasn't doing it any more, but he didn't let me get that out."

With a heated reply he immediately exclaimed, *"No sir! No sir! This is my store and you are not to be putting those things into the grocery bags."* On and on he went, and little by little I was getting frustrated that he would not let me speak.

What could I say? He was right, and I had done wrong.

But as he turned around and started to walk into the large meat cooler, with it's loud blowers going, I quickly, and nervously spoke up and said, *"Well, they're going to Hell."*

He did not hear me say, *"They're."* I have no doubt that he thought I said, *"You're...going to Hell,"* because he said, *"Don't give me that, don't give me that!"*

A few minutes later I was fired from that job. The first job I had ever been fired from. I did odd jobs until the end of the school year. Not long after that, the school year finished, and I had the opportunity to fly back to California for a month.

Back in the mountains of California, I heard the breezes blow through the trees, and felt the cool air. But now I had answers to questions. I had Bible answers to questions, and I wanted to witness to my family and lead them to the Lord.

But the more I witnessed to them, the worse things would get. I would end up preaching, and they would walk away.

Looking back, I wish I would have had the sense to see that the Lord was trying to show me that He did not want me there. But those people, family and friends were on my heart. All I could think was, *"If they don't get saved they are going to go to Hell. Oh, how I want them to know the joy I know."*

Then one Sunday I went down to my old church, First Baptist Church of Sonora. I walked into the auditorium and memories raced through my mind. All night prayer meetings, my baptism, friends, and the trouble that I had gone through there.

I walked in and sat down about three fourths of the way back. A few of my friends were there, and we were having a good time talking and fellowshipping before the service began. All of a sudden, I heard this loud gruff voice in my ear, *"You're in my seat."* I had been talking so it took me by surprise.

The hoary-headed old man snarled again, *"You're in my seat."*

"Oh, I am?" I replied, and immediately I got up out of the seat and stepped to the aisle. Looking behind him I saw four or five seats open, so I moved back a pew and sat down not thinking too much about it. It was still rather early and there were many open seats but, I had supposedly chosen his.

The services began and the hoary-headed old man, in his suit and tie, with his hoary-headed old wife, were sitting right in front of me. They were very dignified, and rather "stuffy" you might say.

There I was, one year of Bible school under my belt. I was charged up spiritually with the word of God. Called to preach, with a fire burning in my soul that was hard to contain.

At school in the church services we would shout, *"Glory to God, Amen, Hallelujah,"* as the old time congregational hymns were sung. 'Amens' were loud and enthusiastic. We were fired up, and I was fired up.

There on that Sunday morning, we stood to sing the old hymn, "Victory in Jesus." Standing there with the rest of that well dressed, dignified congregation, we started to sing. And then I started to shout, "Glory to God, Amen." On and on I went.

I wasn't trying to put on a show, I was glad to be saved, and happy knowing that in Jesus I had the victory.

The "dignified" but gruff old man in front of me ducked when I shouted. He then turned around, glared at me and bellowed, "What? Are you crazy?"

I replied, "No, I'm just happy."

All through the sermon there were times when I would loudly say, "Amen," and the old man would grumble and twitch like he had a burr under his seat.

Finally, the time came to go back to Pensacola, and I was glad when it came. I just wish I would have seen then that things did not go well for me back home, and that the Lord did not want me there. But I did not see that...then.

Back in Pensacola I breathed a sigh of relief. It was a sigh of, *"Thank you, Lord. It sure is good to be back in your perfect will, where you want me to be."*

Needing another job, I immediately set out looking for one. I started on one side of the street and went to every business, putting in applications all along the way. That year I went through eight jobs. Praise the Lord, none of them were because I was fired. But, for one reason or another, they would let me go, and I would have to look for another job.

One of the jobs was working for $2.00 an hour as a mechanic's helper. With my old faded blue VW running again, I wanted to put scripture on it. With masking tape, I marked out the words on the back of the car, *"The wicked shall perish."* (A nice message of love.) Then with a spray can of grey primer, I sprayed primer all over the back of my car. After the primer dried I pulled the tape off and there it was. I had scripture on my car. It was a work of art.

During those days of Pensacola Bible Institute, there were many junkers for cars. One man in my class had a six cylinder car, but it ran on five cylinders. One cylinder was dead, but it got him and his family to and from school.

My car had the front passenger seat out of it, and from time to time I would give people rides to school. It always brought stares when I would pull in to school, and a couple would be sitting in the back seat. But it did make it easier for them to get in and out.

Those days were good days. They were hard days, but fun too. I was twenty-two and single, and thrilled to be serving the King of Kings. But what did the Lord want me to do? Would I be a missionary? Would I be a pastor? These thoughts would continually go through my mind.

When I arrived back in Pensacola from California, I stayed with John again, but things were not working out this time. The Lord then opened up an opportunity to be boarded by a third-year family, Jim and Linda

Smith. They had three children and took me in for a very reasonable price, and I shared a room with their son. The Smith's informed me that I was the third student they had taken in, and since it was kind of a ministry for them, they would pray about whom to have in next when a student left, usually because he got married.

Jim was a third-year student, meaning that this was his last year in school, and he would be graduating. He and his wife, Linda, were praying about where to go after graduation, and one of those prayers was to go back to Pennsylvania and start a church.

Jim decided to take a survey trip to see if the Lord would want them to go back to their home area. There was a two week break at Christmas time. He decided that he would take his family up to Pennsylvania for Christmas and asked me if I wanted to go along.

I said that I would like to go, and we packed our things into his VW bus, and to Pennsylvania we went. Two things would happen on this trip that would show me that the Lord was going to lead me into evangelism.

The first thing was as follows.

It was very cold when we were there. At night it would reach between 10 and 20 degrees below zero. There was snow all around. I was cooped up in the house, and though the people were very friendly, they were people that I did not know.

I had asked if there were any mountains around there, and to my surprise they said that the mountain that I could see from the house was one of the highest mountains around. But to me it was a hill. I was used to real high mountains being that I was from the mountains of California.

One afternoon I set out to climb the mountain that

they had pointed out. The little town of Matamoras set on a flat valley floor with a small river running through it. The trees had all lost their leaves, and their grey branches were covered with a thin layer of snow. The golden yellow sun shown bright, and the light sparkled in the white snow with a backdrop of a clear deep blue sky.

While the crisp cold breeze chilled my nose and watered my eyes, the rest of me was covered with a couple of layers of clothes, boots on my feet, and mittens on my hands.

Across the flat, snowy valley I trudged with my feet sinking into the foot deep snow. It wasn't too far, and I made it to the bottom of the "mountain."

I started up the side of it. It was quite steep, and I would climb with my hands grabbing at small maple trees, and my feet would dig into the side of the mountain snow with the toes of my boots. Up and up I climbed until I reached the top.

There, with the sun shining and warming my face in spite of the cool air, I stood and looked around. Not far in front of me was a monument built out of concrete. It was about five feet high and flat on top, so I climbed up on the monument.

I could see for many miles, and the snow covered hills were a beautiful sight. Thoughts filled my mind. I had worked up a slight sweat, and I was trying to catch my breath.

My mind turned towards the Lord Jesus Christ. *"Lord, what do you want me to do?"* The burden to preach bore down on my being with every beat of my heart. *"Lord, do you want me to be a missionary?" "Lord, what do you want me to do?"*

There standing on that concrete monument, on top

of this small mountain, twenty-two years old, and a little over four years after getting saved, I closed my eyes and prayed. With a little Gideon New Testament in my hands, I prayed and asked, *"Lord, what do you want me to be?"* What I did I do not recommend, but it's what I did.

With my eyes closed I opened the little New Testament, and then holding it in one hand, I put a finger down on it with the other. I then opened my eyes and looked down to the page and verse of scripture that my finger was on. My finger had fallen on the following verse: Acts 26:18 *"To open their eyes, and to turn them from darkness to light, and from the power of Satan unto God, that they may receive forgiveness of sins, and inheritance among them which are sanctified by faith that is in me." I prayed with wonder and asked, "Lord do you want me to be an evangelist?"* It seemed like he did.

I didn't know what to think. I thought to myself, *"Me, an evangelist?"* To me it seemed ludicrous.

I remained on that mountain for a little while longer, and then made my way back to the little home where we were staying. All across the little valley floor smoke arose from the chimneys as people snuggled into their warm and cozy homes. Windows filled with golden light as evening was coming on.

Back at the house I mentioned to Jim about my prayer on the mountain. I then showed him my verse of scripture that the Lord had showed me, and that I thought the Lord wanted me to be an evangelist.

Without hesitation he said to me, *"That verse is a missionary's verse, not an evangelist's verse." "Oh?"* I replied. *"Then I guess the Lord wants me to be a missionary."*

I had been saved less than four years, and to act on what I thought the Lord wanted me to do was something that I knew little about. Sure I did that when I left for school, but Don was for it also, so it wasn't that hard. If Don had been against me going to Bible school, it could have really messed me up and hindered me from doing the will of God.

In my thoughts I was thinking that surely Jim knows the Lord better than I do. He is more experienced and closer to God than me.

So my belief that the Lord wanted me to be an evangelist was short lived. I guess He wants me to be a missionary, and because of what Jim said, I planned and moved in the direction of being a missionary.

Did he mean well? Yes! Was he trying to help me? Of course he was! Was he wrong? Yes! But, at that time I had no confidence in what I thought the Lord wanted me to do. So, for the next year and a half I believed that I would be a missionary.

On the way back to Pensacola, we stopped in Maryland for a New Year's preaching service at a new church that was meeting in a house. The Pastor was Buddy Cargill. That evening the service went on and we preached in the new year.

They called on me to preach, and I got up and preached. It went very well, and at one point, people were standing out of their chairs and shouting. It was one of the first times I had ever preached. It was a very evangelistic service and sermon. I enjoyed being able to preach, but I did not even think about evangelism for I thought that I was a missionary.

We made it back to school and the 'new year' went on getting older. While at school there would often be fellowships at various houses of the students' and couples' that attended the school. At these fellowships, the highlight of the evening was not the food, but the preaching. Various students would come and hope that they would get a chance to preach.

Makeshift pulpits would be erected out of boxes, stacked chairs, or anything that would hold a Bible while the preacher stood and preached. The sermons would vary as much as the personalities of the ones preaching. It was not a sausage factory where everybody looked and talked the same.

Some preachers were newly saved and called to preach. Others were not called to preach but would get up and give a testimony of how they got saved. Some of the sermons were loud and demonstrative while others would be quiet and reserved.

I remember one preacher that as he preached he took off his shoes and held up his foot and yelled, *"These are beautiful feet for the Bible says, How beautiful are the feet of them that preach the gospel of peace, and bring glad tidings of good things!"* Romans 10:15

One Saturday night Jim, his family and I went to one of these fellowships. Our names were put in a hat, and I happened to be one of the ones whose name was drawn to preach.

Quickly, I took a paper plate and scribbled some notes on it from a sermon that I had been thinking about for some days. After the first two preachers, they asked me to preach.

With my paper plate of notes and my Bible, I got behind the makeshift pulpit made up of a small table placed on top of some chairs. It was an older, small house with the old, yellowish light bulbs glowing. People sat on kitchen chairs, the couch, easy chairs, and some stood against the walls.

As I began to preach, the Lord gave me liberty. Preaching very hard and loud, I preached on the subject of getting out of Egypt. (Egypt, in the Bible, is a picture of this world, and Christians are to come out and be separate from the world.) Again, it went very well; people seemed to be touched by the sermon. When we got back home that night, Jim took his TV and threw it out the back door and broke it. He then came up to me and thanked me for the sermon.

These were all signs of what the Lord wanted me to do, and that evangelism was his call for me, but I did not see it. I figured that I was supposed to be a missionary because of what Jim had told me about Acts 26:18 being a verse for missionaries, not evangelists.

I did not have the confidence to believe that what the Lord had shown me was actually just that, the Lord showing me that He wanted me to be an evangelist. If I knew that it was the Lord, then who cares what others may say or think. But I didn't know; I only thought that maybe it was the Lord. So when someone I looked up to had a different opinion, I, without hesitation, embraced their counsel.

One of the first life changing decisions that I made contrary to the counsel of someone I looked up to was that of my wife.

Pensacola Bible Institute was a different sort of school. In those days many of the students were married, and those who weren't married were usually men or young men who had been out in the world with rough backgrounds. Many had been on drugs, booze, and who knows what. But, by the grace of God, they had asked the Lord Jesus Christ to save them, and then on top of that, the Lord had called them to preach.

Some of the students had never finished high school, and others were college graduates. There was a great diversity in the school, except that there were very few single girls. Out of the two hundred or so students, there were seven available single girls. And those seven girls were sought out constantly by one single man or another.

These were young men who had been in the world and had been with women, but were now trying to live right. Some of them weren't desperate for a wife, but it was close to that.

I remember when I was rooming with John. (He is happily married now with a wonderful wife, and they are both serving the Lord.) He had met a girl over the phone, and without ever seeing her in person asked her to marry him. They never did get married. Another young man met a girl on Friday, and asked her to marry him on Sunday. Yes, they got married and are still married.

Another time, John and I had moved out of the roach-infested apartment and ended up in an old single-wide mobile home. Next door to us was another single-wide mobile home with a couple of single girls living in it who were going to Pensacola Bible Institute.

It was a Saturday and I was out in the front yard. One of the girls came over to the chain link fence that separated our yards. She was about nineteen years old and had been saved for a little over a year. As we talked I discovered she was very troubled.

Being single, and a pretty girl, she had been a very popular item at school. Young man after young man had asked her out, and within a year she had been asked to get married at least twice. Well, one of the young men asked her to marry him, and she said yes.

He was a rough character and had come up in a rough, drinking, drug abuse, fighting life.

She had not grown up that way. Though she had not been raised in a Christian home, she did not drink, smoke, or live a wild life. She and he were opposites.

This Saturday morning, with tears running down her cheeks, she told me that she did not have peace about marrying this young man, and she didn't know what to do. The invitations were to go out the next day, and the wedding was not far away.

All I could say to her was that if she did not have peace, and if she did not think that it was God's will to marry him, then she had better not marry him. Not long after that, she called off the wedding. He was heartbroken, and she got a reputation as a heart-breaker.

Marriage was not something that I was thinking about all that much. Sure there were thoughts about whom I would marry, and I even prayed for her before I ever met her, but I was so happy to be in Bible school and serving the Lord that a wife was not at the top of my list of priorities.

I have always believed that if I were in God's perfect will, then, not only would I be pleasing to him, which is most important, but that life and things would work out best, and I would be happiest there. So while at school, I remember seeing a couple of single girls that were not the most attractive girls in the world.

On my knees in prayer, I prayed and said, *"Lord, if you want me to marry one of them, Thy will be done."* I wanted to make sure I was surrendered to His will. His will is more important than what I think because the Lord knows what is best; I do not.

This prayer was not a big deal, I just prayed it one

night to make sure I was surrendered. Mainly I was going about my business of Bible school, and preparing for the ministry.

On Thursday evenings, I had an hour open between classes. Because there was no real place to get alone and pray at home with the Smith family, I would take the opportunity to go to an upper room in the church and pray for an hour.

One evening between classes a young, single girl whom I was acquainted with came up to me and asked if she could pray with me on Thursday night. I didn't mind, nor did I think much about her request. I told her it was alright with me, and Terri and I went to the upper room together and prayed for an hour.

Each Thursday we would pray together. It wasn't long before we were more than friends. More and more we started spending time together.

In prayer I would ask the Lord if she was the one He wanted me to marry. This was a big decision, and one that I hadn't really been thinking about. But now I was thinking about it constantly. What should I do? Whom should I talk to, if anyone?

I wasn't sure whom to talk to, though I should have talked to my pastor. Up to this point, I had not had a pastor to speak of. At least one that believed the word of God and was there to talk to. I had come this far, basically, on my own. The only thing I thought of to do was to call Don back in California. It was not the smartest thing to do, but that is what I did.

The first time I called him I asked him something to the effect of, "What things should I look for in a woman?" He told me to check her teeth. I am not kidding, that is what he told me. He also told me to see if she is organized, for example, can she find things in her purse? There was nothing about does she love the Lord, read her Bible or pray. It was all about practical things he told me to look for.

The next time I saw Terri, I started asking her questions about her teeth. Had she ever had a toothache? A cavity? She looked at me strangely, but said nothing.

I then started asking her if she had a pair of nail clippers in her purse, or other things that I thought she might have. She would reach into her purse and I would see if she had any trouble finding things.

Looking back these were rather dumb things to do, but that is what I did. More and more we grew closer as we continued to pray and read the word of God together. Those were our dates. We went out to dinner only once before we got marrried. We both had very little money, so we would stop by a little pond at night after school and talk.

As it became serious, I prayed earnestly if she was the one for me. About that time, Jim said to me, "Be careful, she will break your heart." So I pulled back a little.

In all fairness though, she was not a heartbreaker. She was young in the Lord, as well as young in age. With so many single men around desperate to get married, she was getting asked out right and left, and getting asked often if she would marry them. She has told me that she felt like a piece of cheese in a rat house.

After Jim said that to me, I pulled back for a few days, but then we were back close again. Praying one day if she was the one for me, the Lord gave me a verse and confirmed it in my heart. Prov. 31:30 *"Favour is deceitful, and beauty is vain: but a woman that feareth the LORD, she shall be praised."* I knew she feared the Lord, and she was attractive as well.

I decided that I would ask her to marry me, but first let me make one more call to Don. Why? Because it was a big decision, and I wanted someone to encourage me in that direction. That is a bad thing, and I still fight it.

So one evening, after classes, I called Don. As I talked to him I told him that I believed it was God's will for me to marry Terri. I never will forget his response for as long as I live. He said to me, "The Lord told me that she is not the one for you."

I couldn't believe my ears. It took me totally by surprise. But what I said next was the right thing. I told him that I didn't care what he said; I knew what the Lord had showed me.

For once, I stood on what I thought the Lord wanted me to do. I didn't doubt or change my mind. I stayed with my decision, and I am glad that I did. As you will read, the years ahead would be very hard years.

We had one of the longer courtships at school which was eight months, and we were married in October on the 17th, 1981. My wife, Terri, was the girl I had talked to that day over the fence who didn't have peace about marrying the other man. How could I have known that I was talking to the very girl that about a year later I would marry?

As it got closer to graduation, I made more and more plans to go to Holland as a missionary. I had prayer cards made up, as well as slides, to put together a slide show for deputation. Deputation is when a missionary travels from church to church to get support to live on when he gets to the mission field.

But the more I moved in that direction, the less

peace I had about the call as a missionary. I had gone forward in church publicly to announce my call as a missionary. I couldn't back out now. So I would look for signs that it was God's will. Little coincidences perhaps, or I would listen for the voice of God to direct me.

Any little thing, and I would magnify it to make it sound like God was really leading me in that direction. Mostly, I was trying to convince myself.

Finally, I had to give up. After much prayer I decided that it was not God's will, and that He had not called me to the mission field.

But where do I go now? What do I do now? I want to preach. An urgency consumed me; I must preach! Lord you have called me to preach, but where do I go? What do you want me to do? These thoughts were constantly on my heart and filled my mind.

I would pray, *"Lord you saved me to serve you. I love you, and this burden to preach won't let me sleep or rest. Lord Jesus, what do you want me to do?"*

Day after day I would wrestle with these questions. Day after day I would bear the pressure and fire in my soul that I must preach! The call, the burden, the desire to preach consumed me to the point that I felt like I would explode.

And then in a sermon, Dr. Ruckman would say, *"Are you surrendered not to preach?"* He would mention that from time to time, and I would go to the altar in the invitation crying, *"Lord if you don't want me to preach, Thy will be done. But why then, Lord, have you put this burning desire in me to preach? It doesn't make sense, but Lord Jesus, I am surrendered, the best way I know how, not to preach if that is Your will."*

I would get up from the altar, and yet the fire still

burned in my soul that I must preach. But, the best way I knew how, I was trying to control it, and wait on Him.

When graduation came, at the end of May 1982, I was depressed. Oh, I was excited to graduate, but at the same time I was literally depressed. I was depressed because I just knew, without a doubt, that the Lord Jesus Christ was coming back very soon, and I would never have the chance to preach.

I would walk around with a long face. My wife, Terri, remembers how I was when I mention it to her. Longfaced and down in the dumps. In my prayer I would say, *"Lord, thank you for letting me graduate, but I don't know why because I know you are going to be back before I get a chance to preach."*

That was twenty three years ago.

Finally, the time had come to graduate. My dad came all the way from California, as well as a couple of friends in the Lord, Pete and Russ. Outside of Don, Russ was the most instrumental in my getting saved. He had been a faithful witness to me. Pete had been saved right at the same time I had, and we had prayed many hours together, as well as gone to church.

There they were, my friends, and my father, all the way from California. Now they were here, at school, where the Lord is real and there is great joy. I thought to myself, *"They will see what is going on and maybe my dad will get saved. And maybe, Russ and Pete will see firsthand how great and marvelous the Lord is and take it all back home and start a church."* That was my hope.

Well, I graduated, and my dad, Russ and Pete all went back to California. School was over, and I had no place to go to serve the Lord. Other men in my class had doors open for them. Some were going off to be missionaries. Others were going off to start churches. And still others had churches vote them in as pastors. But no door opened up for me.

I would come home from work, kneel down in prayer, and cry. Terri would try to comfort me when I came out of the bedroom. Did I need to settle down and wait? Yes! Did I need to relax and trust the Lord? Certainly!

But I was twenty-four years old and called to preach. There was no other reason to live than to serve Him.

The Lord had the reigns in my mouth and was trying to hold me back for my own good. But I was pulling at the reigns, *"Let me go, let me run, how can I keep still? I must preach!"*

In July, my first child was born. A boy, Nathan Aaron McDonald, and what a joy! I was now a father. We were living in a single wide mobile home that had mice in the cupboards, and rats coming through the floor at night. Yellowjackets built nests under the floor which I constantly sprayed, but it was only $80.00 a month. Terri was staying at home with Nathan, and my job was just enough to get us by, with very little extra. By that I mean about $5.00 every two weeks was above our meager budget.

A couple of months before Nathan was born, we had the episode with the rat. We slept in the living room on a hide-a-bed couch. One of those contraptions that are horrible to try to sleep on, but, it was all we had. There was a small consolation for Terri, in that her feet were higher than her head, so the swelling in her feet would go down at night.

One night I awoke to a scratching sound that was coming from the base of the wall and floor of the trailer.

In the morning I looked, and sure enough, there was a good sized hole at the corner of the floor where the wall met. I came up with a brilliant plan to eradicate us of this pesky rat.

Having to make do with what I had on hand, I took a filet knife and securely taped it to the end of a long, wooden broom handle. Now, I had a spear; I thought to myself, *"Tonight I'm going to spear that rat."*

Right on time, in the middle of the night, the scratching started. Terri lay next to me sleeping. It didn't take much for her to fall asleep, being pregnant as she was. Little by little the rat pushed against the thin wall paneling, and I could tell it was just about ready to crawl through. I lay there on my back with the homemade spear resting on my body and gripped in my hand.

I thought to myself, *"Just one more minute and I'll have him."* My hand gripped the homemade spear tighter as I readied to strike with great speed and force. The rat now had his head through the hole. I thought, *"It's time!"* Just as I started to strike, Terri rolled over to me and with a panicked voice yelled, *"Ken, the rat's coming through the wall!"* Surprised at her sudden awakening, I shouted, "Yes, I know!" Jumping up I slammed the spear into the hole, yet the rat had vanished. I never did spear it.

Along with the living conditions, Terri's mother was not making things any easier. She lived just a few miles away and would come over almost every day. She was a strict Roman Catholic so we went together like oil and vinegar. No matter what we did she would criticize us, especially me. From time to time, she and I would have a heated argument over the Pope. She would ride Terri about all sorts of things, making Terri a nervous wreck.

These things, coupled with my ever consuming desire to preach moved me to a decision. We were going to California to help a man start a church. He was already out there and needed help, so we would go and help him. At least we would be away from Terri's mother. Just the thought brought a sigh of relief.

Did I know that the Lord wanted us to go to California? I thought that I did. After all, there was a great need in California, which was commonly referred to as the land of fruits and nuts.

Looking back twenty-three years later, I don't know if it was His perfect will to go or not. Knowing now that I am an evangelist, I would have to say that I don't think it was His perfect will, but it was sure good to get away from my mother-in- law.

Chapter 3

FIRST TRIP OUT

Even though Terri had started her third year of Bible school, I could wait no longer. After much prayer, tears, and fasting, I decided that it was the Lord's will for us to go to California. And so began a pursuit to find God's perfect will for my life that would take thirteen years, thousands of dollars, thousands of miles, and every ounce of strength I had.

It was, and is, a pursuit that is every person's duty, yet few pursue to the final day. God's will for my life, well, there is no other reason to live. The pursuit of God's perfect will for my life has been filled with many mistakes, some of which now appear so "stupid" that it is very humbling to record them in this book. Yet, if the recording of them can help someone else, then praise the Lord for that.

It was the February of 1983 when I decided that we should head out to California. We would help a man in the city of Lodi who was starting a church. What things would we take with us, and what would we sell? The decisions are not easy ones. Furniture and various things have sentimental value, yet to move it 2500 miles is another problem. How would we move our things out there?

At the very start of my pursuit of the will of God, I made a very big mistake. As I was trying to figure out how to go about getting our things out there I then accepted help from my lost, Roman Catholic father-in-law. He offered to loan us the money for movers, and we would then pay him back. Sounds perfectly reasonable, doesn't it?

Along with the loan, we would stay at their house for a couple of weeks in order to save up money for the trip out. Again, this was a big mistake.

As I look back, I see that I was the one working it out in my strength; the Lord was nowhere to be found. When you start using the lost to help you serve the Lord, the Lord's blessing stops immediately, and you are on your own. You are now going in your strength, not His.

Ezra 8:22 For I was ashamed to require of the king a band of soldiers and horsemen to help us against the enemy in the way: because we had spoken unto the king, saying, The hand of our God is upon all them for good that seek him; but his power and his wrath is against all them that forsake him.

Ezra 8:23 So we fasted and besought our God for this: and he was intreated of us.

Even if lost family or friends offer to help you, with no strings attached, it would be wise to pass. Although God is able, and at times he can use the lost to meet His children's needs, yet when He does, you will not have a hand in it at all. It will be all God from start to finish. That way He gets the glory. Gen. 14:23 *"That I will not take from a thread even to a shoelatchet, and that I will not take any thing that is thine, lest thou shouldest say, I have made Abram rich."*

After staying with lost in-laws in order to save up some money, the day finally came for us to head out into the work of God. That is exactly how I looked at it too. I was going to serve the Lord, and serve Him back close to home. I would be able to tell the people back home of how the Lord loved and died for them, and that they could be saved and know the love and joy that I knew.

I was leaving to go set the world on fire for Jesus Christ, and what's more, it would be back home in California. These two thoughts filled my heart and consumed my thoughts. Of course, I was excited about serving the Lord, but add to that the thought of being not too far from home, and I was eager to get going.

With our possessions already shipped by United Van lines, (by the way, the movers cost the same as U-haul would have cost) we packed our Mazda four-door GLC and headed West. Disposable diapers lined the bottom of the back window because they took up less room that way.

Nathan, had a cold, but slept great in the bed we made on the back seat. The motion of the car rocked him to sleep, and the stress and tension he sensed from Terri and I as we stayed with the lost in-laws, was now gone. By the time we reached California, he was over the cold and in much better spirits.

Mile after mile we headed West to enter the service of the Lord Jesus Christ. Every mile closer I became more excited and filled with anticipation. I was like a young child who gets more and more excited as each day gets one day closer to Christmas or his birthday.

I contemplated, *"And to think that less than five years earlier I had been saved. Less than five years, and I was a graduate of Bible School and ready for the ministry."* Well, lets say that I thought that I was ready. The Lord knew that I had a lot to learn, and He also knew that for me, I would need the school of hard knocks to learn it in.

I could critique religion, Greek manuscripts, people, and anything else you asked me. I had the answer to any question put to me, or at least I thought I did. The Bible knowledge I had in me was like a loaded gun. Anything that moved wrong I would aim, pull the trigger, and fire. Tact? What's that? My attitude was that if people got offended from the truth then they just needed to get saved, or get right with God. For me, the trumpet had sounded and it was, "Chaaaarrge!"

We headed west as Terri eagerly looked out the windows. The southern landscape of large, green, oak trees with moss hanging off the branches, and pecan and Mamosa trees under a sky of billowy thunder clouds gave way to a much more arid landscape. Short, bushy mesquite trees and tumble weeds lined the highway as barren, rocky mountains began to break into the horizon. She felt her skin and the inside of her nose dry out from the arid surroundings.

Finally, the sign that read, "California." We were just outside of Blythe, California on Highway 10. When we stopped to eat, Terri marveled at the quality of the produce in her green salad; she loved it! I said to her with a big grin, *"Welcome to California."*

Even as I write this, I can remember the excitement that filled me. The thought of having a reason to live, which was to serve the Lord Jesus Christ, to preach the Holy Word of God, and to win people to the Lord Jesus Christ satisfied me with purpose of life like never before. Not just to win any people to the Lord, but the people of Northern California.

Finally, after four days of driving, we began our ascent higher and higher up into the Sierras. I motioned to Terri, "Look!," and there was the sign for the turn-off to Twain Harte. Terri exclaimed, *"Finally, it is real! I've heard so much about this place, and now I can see it."*

We pulled into my home town of Twain Harte. I once again enjoyed the feel and smell of the cool, Fall air which was scented as it whistled through the needles of the tall pines and incense Cedar trees. I took a deep breath, listened to the sound and thought of the need for the gospel to be preached in these hills.

What could be better? I would be serving the Lord, and it would not be too far from here. There was no other thought, nor desire than to preach in this area. To me, this was my mission field.

We arrived at "Grandma T's" house; family came over and we had a great time. When we first walked into the house, Nathan was immediately greeted by family. Since he was their first grandchild, he was the main attraction.

Having come from Florida, all Nathan had known for a house was the small mobile home that we had lived in, and then a short time with in-laws. Now, as Terri and he met family, we walked into the living room.

It was a large room with a vaulted ceiling that was two and a half stories high at the apex.

Nathan looked up and started jibbering with the binky in his mouth. Then he started pointing at the ceiling. I thought of how it will be when we come into the throne of God, looking in indescribable amazement, like Nathan in this large room.

After most of the family had left, I walked onto the deck which was on the back side of the house and about ten feet off the ground. Tall pine and cedar trees grew all around and towered over the porch and the house. Between the large trunks of the trees, I looked towards a mountain that rose to five thousand feet high.

The cool breeze blew across my cheeks. I drank in the moment and then imagined preaching in those hills. I imagined having a camp meeting with great preachers coming and preaching. I imagined souls getting saved, and God doing a great work in those hills. I imagined my family getting saved and coming with me to Heaven.

These were imaginations, dreams, and desires that filled my heart and soul. This was my desire, my purpose, my passion, and it consumed my every being.

We left the mountains and headed to the Central Valley of California to work with Bro. Smith and his wife. They graciously let us stay with them even though they had four children. They also were going through hard times financially, and the church was not getting started all that smoothly.

From the move, we were all very tired, but especially Terri, as she was still nursing, and Nathan was in the same room with us.

One night about 3:00A.M., Nathan started crying continuously because he was hungry. Realizing this I groggily said to Terri, *"Nathan is crying; he's hungry."* She replied, *"I know; I have him."* She was sitting up in bed rocking, and nursing a pillow.

These were hard times, but we had been told that if you are going to serve the Lord then expect hard times, which is good advice. Having never served the Lord out on our own, we did not know whether the hard times were a trial, or some light from God trying to direct our steps into a different direction.

I scoured the city looking for a job, but nothing was turning up. Money was scarce, food was scarce, I had no trade, and the cost of living was very high.

In spite of all this, we officially started having church services on Sundays in Bro. Smith's house. Week after week went by and only a couple of kids would come to the services. I think they were related to the Smith's, and the parents dropped them off, in essence, to be babysat while they did their own thing.

As far as I knew, I was in God's perfect will, but things were getting a little desperate. I needed to get to work, and a place of my own.

I had never been in a situation like this before in my life. I had always been able to get a job, and I was willing to do anything that I needed to do in order to take care of my family. Things were not coming together very well.

I was confused about what to do and decided to call Don, the man that discipled me and was my old boss. He talked me into selling combs again, and going back on the road as a salesman.

I did not want to do this as it would take me out of the area, away from my family during the week, and I would be no help in witnessing for the church.

There would be other times like this in my life. And, during times like this, when I would seek counsel from others, I would have no answers to their logic. Even though in my heart something did not seem right, yet

I was confused and at the end of my rope, so I would listen to the advice and seem helpless to disagree.

During school the Lord had showed me that He did not want me to sell combs, but now, here I was, right back selling combs.

It did help us get into an apartment, and we were able to get on our feet a little. But the time away from Terri was not good. She was home alone with Nathan all day, all night, and I would be gone for four and five days at a time. Mrs. Smith would come over now and then, but she was busy with her own life and family.

Terri with her young, firstborn son was all alone, in a new town, not knowing anyone. The first class in the school of hard knocks was about to have a test.

Don would tell me where I ought to go to sell. Each week it got farther and farther away. I didn't like it, but I didn't know what else to do.

I left on a trip that headed south, working my way from Bakersfield down to El Centro, California, about six hundred miles away, almost to the Mexican border. On this certain day, the pressure started to get to me. Even though I was praying and reading my Bible, burdens were beginning to consume me.

The customers could sense it for my sales began to fall. Away from my family, bills coming in, the bottom falling out of my sales, and the church not doing well, all arose in me a fear that I could not quench, and I began to panic. I thought to myself, *"What am I going to do?"* I must do something! A worried reasoning pressed me, *"Don doesn't know what he is talking about."*

I was in Tehachapie, California, heading south, and becoming more and more panicked by the minute. My faith was well nigh gone, and great fear was replacing it. It was then and there that I made a very big mistake. A mistake that still hurts to this day.

When a sheep gets scared it panics and runs with no thought as to where it's running to, or what it is doing. That was me that day. Up to that point, looking back, I believe I was in the will of God. Now, that was all going to change.

My mind was on the Lord. God what should I do? God what have I done wrong? How am I going to pay my bills?

I pulled out the map and looked. Just on the other side of the mountains I knew of another preacher. He had a church in Tujunga, California. I gave him a call, and he said to come on over, there were plenty of stores to sell to, and they would love to have me.

Let me say this before I go any farther. This man was doing a good job, had a heart for God, and he tried to help me.

I headed for Tujunga, a place where it seemed like they had all the answers. This was refreshing to me, as I was out of answers, and those whom I had been listening to weren't helping me, or so I thought.

Pulling into Tujunga, they greeted me, and refreshed my spirit. After a couple of days of working there, sales began to pick up. I then talked to them about all that I had been through, how things were going, and what I should do?

Of course, they had the answers. I should come and help them in the ministry there. They said that it would be an answer to prayer since they had been praying for help. That sounded real good to me as I thought that it was possible that the Lord had led me to them. Maybe it was God's will.

I called and told Terri who was a bit surprised, yet

it seemed to sound good to her, as things did not seem to be working out up there.

Arriving back in Lodi I had to tell Bro. Smith. It was something that I did not look forward to doing. Here was a man who was trying to start a church, and had to a certain extent, who still depended on me for help. It still bothers me when I think of the day that I told him that I would be moving to Tujunga, California. He looked like he had been kicked in the stomach. But I had made up my mind; we were moving to Tujunga.

What we were really doing was moving out of the will of God. I know this now without a doubt; I know now that this move was not of God, and that the Lord Jesus Christ did not direct me to move there. It was a move generated out of fear, not the Holy Spirit. Almost always, decisions made out of fear are the wrong decisions.

I was trying with all my heart to do right, to please the Lord, and to fulfill his will for my life. His will! That prize, that goal, that lofty duty, that aspiration drove me daily and would not let me go. Ever onward, pressing on. I must do the will of God for my life.

I had never been out of God's will up to that point in my saved life. I got saved, grew in the Lord, and then went to Bible school. It was all so simple then. But now simplicity was gone and replaced with fear and confusion. To the best of my ability, I thought that I was doing the right thing, and that it was God's will. But, in eight horrible months I would come to realize that I was so wrong.

What follows is an example of what happens when you are trying to do right, but out of God's perfect will. It was a time, a memory, that I do not enjoy writing about.

We loaded up our things again. (Just a short statement, but a lot of work along with much anguish.) Our second move in six months, and in those six months we had been in a place of our own for two months.

Upon arrival in Tujunga, our first week or two was a honeymoon period, with things going alright. The arrangement was that I would be supported part-time from the church, and that I would work the rest of the time as a salesman in the Los Angeles area.

Rent was $750.00 a month. (That made a lot of sense, going from $275.00 to $750.00 because I was worried about how I was going to pay my bills.)

Right from the start my wife started taking the brunt of things. This would be an all out attack before it was over to get Terri to quit on the Lord. She has been a great wife and stayed with the stuff over the years, but this first battle was going to be a very rough one.

It started off that her job was to watch the nursery during church services. Since Nathan was in the nursery, it seemed to make sense. The problem was that she was always in the nursery, or at least ninety percent of the time. Most of the time with no break of someone else taking a turn so she could sit in the services. If she asked to sit in the services so she could get some preaching, she was jumped on as complaining, and it was implied that she was not right with God.

During this first month or so, we were staying with people, and both of us were sleeping on a single bed together, with Nathan in the same room again.

As far as my part-time position at the church, it turned into more than part time with part-time pay. Along with this, I was always being watched to see if I was doing my job. The honeymoon was over, and the nightmare had just begun.

How much to go into, I'm not sure. I will give you one of the worst stories of that time.

We had been staying with people before we could get into an apartment of our own. Then a couple from the church was leaving for Bible school. This would open up an apartment for us to stay in. Praise the Lord! We will have a place to stay in of our own. Sounds simple doesn't it?

Much of the area we were in was not all that good. Helicopters were often overhead at night with search lights on looking for criminals running from the cops. Drugs were evident all around. This small apartment complex was one of the few that was decent to live in. It was single story, stair stepped on a hill. Two apartments, then a step up to another two apartments, totaling about ten apartments all together.

When this couple left for Bible school, we told the landlord that we would rent out the apartment which she gladly agreed to. But there was one problem. The pastor, who lived in the apartment next to it, wanted that apartment because it had a tree in the yard. He was adamant that he wanted the apartment for the tree.

But what about us? He told me that we could take his apartment. Well, that was okay. with me, except for one thing. The pastor had a little dog, and while living there, they would not clean up after that little dog. So there had been dog dung all over the floor from that little dog.

The landlord said that if the pastor moved into the other apartment, she would not also clean the pastor's apartment for us to move into. We would be paying

$750.00 on a cleaning deposit for an apartment that wasn't clean.

Terri, as the good mother that she is, was concerned about her son on a floor that had been filthy, as well as seeing us getting the short end of the stick.

During this time my mind was so full of confusion that I couldn't even see what was right or wrong. That may sound strange, but that is how I was. This was the preacher, and though the deal before us was not right, yet he was the preacher and my boss, and what was I to do? We didn't have classes that covered this sort of thing at school.

This was the school of hard knocks, and this was a very hard knock.

Terri was giving me her complaint, and I will say, rightfully so, but I did not know what to do. Was I to buck the pastor?

It all finally boiled over in a meeting with pastor, his wife and us, when Terri mentioned to them that the apartment wasn't even clean. That is when the preacher blew up on her, his wife also got all over her, and I stood there like a dunce. How it hurts to write this now. I know what I would do now. But, I didn't know what to do then.

Terri just cried as they rebuked her unjustly. If it had not been for her love for the Lord Jesus Christ, and her daily Bible reading and prayer, she never would have made it through this. I will say that Satan, through that preacher and his wife did all that the Lord allowed him to do to get her to break.

The main problem though was that we were not in the perfect will of God, and the Lord was trying to show us. The Devil was also trying to bust up our marriage and get us to quit so that we would never fulfill God's will for our lives.

That's it! God's will! God's desire for our lives, my life, Terri's life, and Nathan's. God's will, that lofty apex of achievement. But what was God's will for me now? I thought I was in the will of God.

Terri lost some respect for me that day. She felt betrayed and all alone. For her, Tujunga was a living Hell with no relief in sight.

Terri and I ended up renting the pastor's dirty apartment. We rented a rug cleaner and cleaned the house ourselves. Well, it mainly fell on Terri as the pastor called me away from the house so I wasn't even there. If I complained, then I was rebuked for it. It had been about eight months since leaving Bible school, and we were just getting into a place of our own. Unfortunatley, it looked like we would be there a while.

During this time of being out of God's will, it didn't matter what we did, it was always wrong. If we liked one thing, they liked another, and we were looked upon as backslidden because of it.

Little by little we would escape to the mountains on the Angeles Crest highway. It was a highway that climbed the mountains right behind Tujunga. Up on top there were pine trees, the breeze blew, and it was a break from the nightmare called Tujunga.

One of the best things I did during this time was to start reading a book called, War on the Saints by Jesse Penn Lewis. It was a book about how Satan will attack a saint. There is one thing that stood out in the book, and it was this:

Satan will work on a Christian and get him or her to a point where they are spiritually paralyzed. By that the author meant that you can get to a point where you are so afraid of making a mistake that you will listen for a voice, or look for a sign as to what God wants you to do. You yourself, though, are incapable of making any decisions on your own. You are paralyzed.

When I read it, I knew that was me. I was afraid of everything. In my head my daily thoughts and contemplations were intense, but I had no answers as to what to do.

The book said that if you are in such a state, you must force yourself to make decisions. Decide to the best of your ability what is right, and then decide to go in that direction. That was the answer I needed. I knew without a doubt that I needed to do that.

There was just one problem, how do I stand up to pastor? He already looks at me as if my wife is running me, and that I am backslidden.

He was a slick talker. One of the men in the church said that, *"Pastor could sell a refrigerator to an Eskimo."* How would I deal with him? I had no answer, but I was getting desperate.

By now the impression that I was not in the will of God was getting through. I had never been out of the will of God before in my saved life, but in my mind I thought that this sure seemed like what it would be like when you get out of the will of God. Pastor said that I was a quitter, and turning my back on God.

I would go out selling during the day and then return straight to the church. When no one was there, I would kneel at the altar for one to two hours a day, crying, and asking the Lord to help me get out of there.

After a couple weeks of this, one late afternoon, I was at the church altar when the pastor walked in. I was in tears, and deeply broken. Startled I got up. He looked at me and said that if it was that bad, then maybe I needed to leave. I agreed, and relief flooded my soul. Thank you Lord for taking care of having to deal with the pastor. Let's get out of here!

Where do I go Lord? What is your perfect will? There it is again, the will of God. That lofty aspiration, that duty, that privilege for sinful man to perform. I had no idea where to go, just to get out of there.

I knew though that I must make a decision. I must decide to the best of my ability what the Lord wanted me to do. I might be wrong, but at least half of the decision would be right, I would be out of here, and I knew that much was right!

After calling a few christians for advice, it seemed that I should go back to the last place where I was in the will of God. Where was that? Pensacola? Lodi? I did not know.

I decided that we would take a survey trip and go back up to Northern California. I would look for a job. We would stay at Grandma T's, and I would go to Modesto and look for a job. I would line up the interviews, and I would look all day. If a job came open, then I would take that as God's will that He wanted us to move back up there. If I did not get a job, then I would take that as God's will that He wanted us back in Pensacola, Florida.

We went back home to the mountains, and I looked for work all over the place. There were no restrictions on my applications; I would say "yes" to whatever came along. One place said to come back at 3:00P.M. I applied all over town, but nothing was coming in.

In the afternoon I stopped by to say hello to Don, who was in Modesto at that time. We talked for a bit, but when it came time for me to leave for the 3:00P.M. appointment, he said to me, "Don't go, stick around and fellowship." I listened to him. That was the last appointment I had scheduled for the day. I had gone to every other appointment with that one being the last one.

I always think of this day when I read Judg. 19:7 *"And when the man rose up to depart, his father in law urged him: therefore he lodged there again."* I stayed and fellowshipped with Don, and never went to the appointment assuming they probably wouldn't hire me anyway. The Lord wants us back in Pensacola. Oh My! How foolish can you be?

We left the mountains and headed back to Tujunga to pack once again and head for Florida. On the way South we stopped on the Grapevine, a mountain range separating the Central Valley of California from the Los Angeles Basin. Looking towards the north we felt peace inside. Then facing south towards Tujunga we felt turmoil.

I remember saying to Terri, *"Why do we feel this way? What is the Lord trying to tell us?"* I did not know. All I knew was that I had to make a decision, whether right or wrong, I new we had to get out of Tujunga, and the last place I knew, absolutely, that I was in God's will was Pensacola, Florida. Pensacola, here we come.

We arrived back in Tujunga and started to pack. Our name was mud. To them, we were backslidden and couldn't take the ministry. *"His wife won out, and he is run by his wife." "God will never use Ken McDonald."* We heard all of these accusations.

All we were trying to do was to serve our Lord Jesus Christ. We were trying our best. We were trying to do God's will for us. Ah, there it is again. That illusive treasure. We had listened to all of the advice, and it didn't work for us. (Now I know why, at the time I did not.)

In the eyes of those at the church, those that we had tried to serve and minister to, we were quitters and failures.

In a year and a half, we went from a couple that was excited about the opportunity to serve the Lord, with hearts only wanting to help others and glorify the Lord Jesus Christ, to a couple that was defeated, discouraged, exhausted, and wondering if God even knew we were alive.

Chapter 4

BACK TO PENSACOLA

The day that I thought would never arrive, finally did. It was October 31st, 1983, Halloween. We were packing our things and eagerly anticipating our move away from Tujunga.

The pastor, who had his apartment with the tree in the front yard, now viewed us with disgust, and his attitude affected most of the church. But that day there was a man, who was a great blessing to me, whom I will never forget. Bro. Ed Butler, an older, but strong retired man, came by to help us move the heavy things. No one else but Bro. Butler came by to help us. There were some large items that we had to move out of the apartment, but there was no place for us to leave them. He came by and took them off our hands, and I am sure he had no idea what a blessing from the Lord he was to us that day. I knew the Lord had sent him to us.

It was around 10:00 P.M. when we, though very tired, excitedly pulled out of Tujunga, California and headed back to Pensacola, Florida. Terri had a smile on her face, and we both rejoiced to be getting out of there. Though it was getting late at night, we determined that even if we got a few hours distance away from Tujunga, that it would be well worth it.

Pensacola was the last place that I knew I had been in God's will. God's will! I had to be in God's will. I just knew that if I was in God's will everything would be alright. I knew that God's will was the reason I was alive, and that I must fulfill God's will for my life. If I had gotten out of His will then all I knew was to go back to the last place where I knew I had been in His will. Cost and sacrifice were irrelevant. What mattered was, as Paul asked, *"Lord, what wilt thou have me to do?"*

This was now my third move in about a year, and including this move, I would have moved over 5,000 miles, spent a few thousand dollars, and ended up right back at the beginning.

Terri was beat down, as well as I. We were worn, exhausted and felt like failures.

Terri's mother would always call us on the weekends, so she knew that we were coming back to Pensacola. Being the slow learner that I am, I let her find us a place to stay. (Don't use lost family. Yes, there may be exceptions, but the Lord usually does not bless it.) I had not learned that lesson yet, so we were in for more trouble.

We arrived back in Pensacola and went to where our new residence would be. It was a long single-wide mobile home, which was situated under the long, arching branches of large, southern oak trees. It was a very shaded, dark and damp place.

The trailer had holes in the floor where you could see through to the outside ground. This was not all that unusual for Pensacola, but what was worse was the smell that would emanate up through those holes in the floor.

Making the best of the situation, we got busy cleaning the trailer as best as we could before our things arrived with the movers.

A couple of days later, our things arrived, and when the large moving truck came down our street, it got stuck in the ditch on the side of the street. After hours of delay, a large tow truck came and barely winched it out. I write this because it was an event that would later help me see that Pensacola was not God's perfect will for us, though at this time I did not know that. I actually thought that I was in His will.

Our earthly possessions were finally put away, and we settled into our smelly single wide mobile home. We were literally dazed, weary, perplexed, and confused from all that had happened to us in little over a year. That year was to us a year of failures. We had gone from one failure to another. We were discouraged and very low in spirit. We were accused of not being right with God, not being tough enough to handle the hard times, and not ever being useful for God. In our minds we thought that maybe they were right. Maybe we just don't have what it takes.

One day, not long after arriving back in Pensacola, Terri was riding in a car with one of her close friends, Holly Wilson. Holly had been Terri's maid of honor at our wedding.

Riding along with Holly driving, Terri's eyes filled with tears. She then asked, *"Holly, do I look backslidden? Do I look like I've gotten away from God?"*

Holly looked at her and said, *"No Terri, not at all."* Tears flooded her eyes for though she had tried to do her best, yet she had heard nothing but the opposite for the last six months.

I will say that we were very dazed from it all.

I remember one evening, a few days after we arrived back in Pensacola, a brother in the Lord who had been in my class at Bible school called me. His name was Alan Cole. We were friends in school, and he had come down to Pensacola from Ohio on business for his father. I think it was something to do with farming. Our conversation went something like this:

Me, in a low, depressed, emotionless voice, *"Hello?"*

Alan, in a friendly, energetic voice, *"Ken, this is Alan, Alan Cole."*

Me, in a low, unexcited, monotone reply, *"Hi."*

Alan, perplexed, *"Don't you remember me from school?"* (After all, it had only been a little over a year.)

Me, stilll in a low, monotone, emotionless reply, *"Yes, I remember you."*

Alan, seeming to be a little upset, *"Well...bye"*.

Me, *"Bye"*.

That was it. I was beat up from inside to outside. We were broke, and nothing was going right.

We went to church, and it was good to walk into the building. It seemed like a place of refuge. There were many familiar faces, and it was good to see them, but we were not the same, and I think it showed.

Sitting down in the pew we just kind of stared into space and tried to let the fog clear. Our minds and spirits were numb from the trials that had befallen us in the past year. During the preaching I tried to say 'amen,' but it seemed to fall to the ground.

After church, Terri was talking to a lady who

introduced her to another young lady.

"This is Terri McDonald."

The lady, having heard of Ken and Terri McDonald from the gossip grapevine replied, *"Oh, you're Terri McDonald."* Terri knew immediately what the reply meant for she was friends with people in Tajunga. In some circles, even here, our name was mud. But all we were trying to do was to serve the Lord and to do right. It was like we were lying on the ground with the wind knocked out of us, and now and then someone would kick us again.

The temptation was to get our eyes on those people, but it wasn't those people that were the problem. The Bible says, Eph. 6:12 *"For we wrestle not against flesh and blood, but against principalities, against powers, against the rulers of the darkness of this world, against spiritual wickedness in high places."*

It wasn't people; it was a spiritual battle that we were in, and we were fighting it the best way we knew how. To get our eyes on the people would have meant sure death spiritually. My issue was not with those people, it was with God, and what His will for my life was. That is all that mattered, and it is all that still matters.

Some how I knew that if I was not in God's perfect will then things would not go well, and, if it was people that were giving me a bad time, it really wasn't them, but rather the Lord showing me that I was not in His perfect will.

So, in a strange way, the trouble, or hurt that was caused by those people was a blessing in disguise for it did not let us get comfortable when we were out of God's perfect will.

About a week after being back in Pensacola, my

brother called from California. He told me that a construction company had called him looking for me. They wanted to hire me. It was the construction company that I had an interview with, but failed to go to as I stayed talking to Don.

It's hard to explain how I felt when he told me the news of the job. I was immediately aware that I had failed again. How could I be so stupid and not finish the job I had to do? I had let a man, a good friend, Don, stop me from finding, and being in the Lord's will.

The school of hard knocks was just that, hard knocks.

So I would have had a job if I would have finished my interviews that day. That would have been the answer that it was God's will for us to be there, but I had failed on my end. We would have avoided this whole trip back to Pensacola. There was no way at this time to even consider going back to California.

Discouraged, depressed and all-around weary, I just got a job and settled in where I was, or at least I tried to.

The smell in the trailer was getting worse. At times it was almost unbearable. After a month or so of trying to figure out what it was, I checked under the trailer and discovered that our sewage was dumping out on the ground.

We called the landlord, a lost Roman Catholic who was a friend of Terri's Mom. (Again don't use lost family or friends.) He would not help us. He said that he had already had it fixed. Terri was crying from the smell for she had to smell it all day long. She prayed, *"Lord, help, what do we do?"*

Thank God for mercy! A quaint little country house

opened up that was affordable. We moved in, and it gave us the much needed help emotionally. Out in the country, a clothes line, and a real house. A single family home. That was around December, and then it got cold. Real cold, and the house was not insulated. The heating bills were "through the roof," and we didn't have enough money to pay them.

We had been back in Pensacola about four months, and I began to think that we were not in God's will. With my brother's phone call about the construction company, I thought that I really had missed the mark. But Lord, what do I do now? Do I go back out to California?

I started praying about this, and it seemed like we weren't in God's perfect will in Pensacola. The Lord seemed to be showing me that He wanted us in California. But we didn't have any money; how would we get back out there?

Well, there was only one way and that was to sell everything. We were basically out of debt, which was a plus. So the only thing was to sell everything, head back out to California, and get back into the will of God. After all, there is nothing more important other than your walk with God, and that walk is at its best in His will.

My attitude is that it is a privilege to serve the Lord. I deserve Hell. He bought me with His blood, and Lord, Thy will be done. It wasn't God's fault that I messed up; it was my fault. It was only right that I should do all that I could to get where He wanted me to be.

I told Terri that I thought that we needed to move back to California. She asked, *"But how?"* And I told her that we would sell everything that we had. (Terri is going to get much gold up in Heaven.) She agreed, and thought also that it was the Lord's will for us to be out in California.

We had a yard sale and sold all that we had. When that was done I went to Dr. Ruckman's office and told him what we were doing. I told him that we were out of debt, that we had sold everything, and that I believed the Lord wanted us out in California.

It was such a blessing to see his reaction. He got a blessing out of our determination and encouraged us in our pursuit.

It had been so long since someone encouraged us in the service of the Lord Jesus Christ. Then to my surprise, the church gave us a $500.00 check for the trip.

There seemed to be light starting to shine where for so long it had been darkness.

Chapter 5

BACK TO CALIFORNIA

Six months in Pensacola, and we were leaving. The decision had been made, and we started to see the Lord work some things out for us. One of the first was the generous gift from the church.

News that we were leaving was announced from the pulpit by Dr. Ruckman when he gave a testimony of what we were going to do. He mentioned that we were out of debt, and that we had sold everything. He also told of how it was a rare thing for him to see a family that had been through what we had been through go back out into the fight.

So now it was out. The McDonald's were going back out to Modesto, California. That was the town where the construction company was that had offered me the job, so I took it from the Lord that that was where I needed to be.

As soon as the service ended that morning, a couple, sitting in the pew right in front of us, turned around and asked about Modesto.

"Did we hear right? That you are moving out to Modesto, California?"

I told them that they had heard right. They then asked where we were going to stay, and I told them that I did not know as we had not gotten that far in our plans yet.

"Well, we have some close friends out there, right in Modesto, and they would probably let you stay with them."

Thank you Lord! I started to see the hand of God working in our lives again.

They gave us the name of these people, Anthony and Cindy Delfin. (We have been close friends with this family ever since.) We now had a contact.

That evening, in the church service, a missionary spoke and presented his call to the mission field. After the service, the Lord seemed to put it on my heart to help the missionary, so I gave him $350.00, which was about all that was left, after tithe, of the $500.00 we had received from the church. We still had enough money to get out there, but that was it. I also wanted to make sure that I was trusting the Lord.

You may think that it was a needless sacrifice. Maybe, maybe not. Either way it was a step of faith.

Again we left for California. By now, with the encouragement from the Lord, we were in much better spirits. What little we had, our clothes, a few pots and pans, and other odds and ends, we packed into the Mazda GLC and headed West. I had a few books that we sent book rate through the post office. Half of them never made it out there, and I never saw them again. If there had ever been any respect from Terri's mother it was completely gone by now.

She had never been too fond of me anyway. Now, to her, I was a stupid fool that she wished more than ever had never married her daughter. I did not care. What mattered to me was being faithful to my Lord, and His will for my life.

On this move there was no help whatsoever from lost relatives. It was a move by faith in God and that was it. I only wish I would have learned this lesson at this time. It would have kept me out of a bunch of trouble in the future.

This was our third 2500 mile move in two years. We never really minded the road. Now that we are in evangelism I know why. In a way the road seemed right to us, but we did not know why at the time.

We crossed the California line again, and headed north. Ah yes, California! Great produce, great weather, and best of all for us, God's will.

I took a deep breath and thought to myself, "Smell that air; that is the peaceful smell of the will of God!"

Partly because of the nightmare of memories of the Los Angeles, Tujunga area, we cut up the eastern side of the mountains and avoided the Los Angeles basin altogether. As I went by the turnoff that would have taken us over the Angeles Crest highway, the highway that seven months earlier we would drive up to escape the nightmare we were in. I faked like I was going to turn onto it. I was joking around, and yet so glad to be out of there.

When I did though, Terri jumped with fear, and I saw again how much pain she had gone through. It had been a nightmare for us all, but especially for her.

To be out of God's perfect will opens you up to more attacks from the Devil, as well as from the world and the flesh. The attacks will almost always be aimed at the weakest point, and that is the woman because she is the weaker vessel.

These attacks come at all times, even in the will of God. Adam and Eve were in God's perfect will, yet the attack came on the woman. It's just that out of God's will, it is much worse.

To our left, and west of us on the other side of those mountains, was a valley that we were going to bypass. The nightmare, the trial, the turmoil that took place in that valley was now behind us. It was a lesson and a test from the school of hard knocks. It was a test that we went through and passed, by the grace of God.

The reason I say that we passed is because we were still in the fight. By God's grace we were not bitter towards God, we were still pressing on for the prize of the high calling of God for our lives. We were pressing on for that will, God's perfect will for our lives. It was and is our duty. And by the grace of God we will not stop until we find His perfect will, get in it, and do what He wants us to do in His perfect will. There is no other purpose in this life than that.

That is why I am alive, to serve Him, to be pleasing to Him, and for Jesus Christ to receive pleasure from me. Rev. 4:11 *Thou art worthy, O Lord, to receive glory and honour and power: for thou hast created all things,* (including me) *and for thy pleasure they are and were created.*

It had been a test to teach us God's will for our lives. It was a test to teach us what it is like to be out of God's perfect will, even though you are trying to do right. It was a test to teach us how to deal with the brethren, which is a test all must pass if they are to do anything for the Lord Jesus Christ.

You must look beyond the brethren and see the hand

of the Lord Jesus Christ. You must keep your eyes on the Lord in spite of the brethren. After all, they are only sinners, and what's more, the Lord is trying you to see what is in your heart, or you might say, He is showing you what is in your heart, and making you deal with it.

It was a test to see if either of us was going to quit on the Lord when things got rough.

We learned many things from that detour out of the Lord's will; unfortunately, there would be more tests ahead in the school of hard knocks.

The Lord allows you to fall and flounder for awhile. He will allow you to fail. A child only learns to walk by falling down, or stumbling before he has the ability to walk.

So too, in the race to run for Jesus Christ, there are times when you will fail and fall. How you respond depends on what you were before you fell down. It is in the failures that your heart is revealed.

If you become angry and bitter, then it is a sign of pride, and that you have a heart that is not surrendered and right with your Savior who bought you with His blood. If you repent and are broken, if you get up and go on, it is a sign of love for God, a sign of charity. *Charity...endureth all things.* 1 Cor. 13:7

We arrived in Modesto, California and went to the Delfin's house. They would let us stay there until we got established in a place of our own. What a blessing they were to us. They did not even know us, yet they let us stay with them.

The day we arrived, Nathan got the chicken pox, and subsequently gave them to Sarah, their little girl of about three years old, and then to their son Joseph who was less than a year old. What a thing! You open up your house to strangers, and they come with chicken pox.

By the time we arrived in Modesto, we had $80.00 left to our name. I had some stocks that had been given to me by Grandma "T", so I put them up for sale. They were worth about two thousand dollars.

When the stock finally sold, I got rebuked sharply by family, but I did not care. I knew I was in God's will, so I would do whatever it took to make it there. God's will was what mattered, not some rainy day nest egg. Jesus Christ and the promises in the word of God are my rainy day nest egg.

I kept holding on to the $80.00 though. It was all I had, and I held on to it kind of like a little child's security blanket. The problem was that two of the tires on our car had steel belts showing. They were worn out, and what was I going to do? The other two tires were not so bad.

I prayed about it and decided to get a couple of new tires. That sounds simple and obvious doesn't it! But when you have a family, no job, and living in someone else,s house, spending your last $80.00 is a major decision.

I spent the money and got the new tires, leaving us with a couple of dollars left. Concern, fear and a good amount of stress compassed me about. Oh, sure, I know, you should be more spiritual and trust the Lord. I was trusting the Lord, or else I never would have done it.

It's amazing how people will tell you how you ought to be, but they have never done what you are doing.

The very day I bought those two new tires the Lord blessed. It had been a week or so since we had seen the Lord do something for us, but that day He gave us $250.00 AFTER I had bought the new tires. I had stepped out by faith, wondering if my foot would rest in quick sand, yet the Lord let it come down on a rock and a firm foundation...faith!

I saw the Lord work that day in my life, and it is a day and a lesson that I will never forget. Many times since then there have been close times and money has been scarce. Memory of that day has helped me to step out in spite of the fear, to trust Him, and let my foot come down on the solid ground of faith.

You must learn to trust the Lord, NOT MONEY!!! You must learn to look through the eye of faith in your heart, not the eye of sight in your head.

The job market was kind of slow, so I went to the unemployment office and applied. It was something that I had never done in my life. In a day I had a job at Valley Copy Service. Not long after that, the stocks sold and, after tithe, we were able to get into a one bedroom apartment.

The Lord had established us! We had not used lost family or lost friends. There was no pulling of strings or working it out in our own power. The Lord had worked it out, and it was a joy to see Him work for us.

No, it wasn't a house. No, it wasn't fancy. Yes, we were sleeping on the living room floor on a piece of foam rubber. But we were in God's will. We knew we were in God's will, and we were back in the battle. We had food and clothes, and were to be content with that.

Yes, the trials were hard. Yes, it was a lot of work. Yes, it was a lot of tears. But what a joy to have the assurance that we were in the will of God, His perfect will, and to have the peace that goes with that knowledge.

How did we know we were in His will? By the mistakes we had made, that is how. If we had gotten mad at God and quit, we never would have made it back to God's will. God's will; that is why you are alive! To do His will for your life!

We settled into our new life in Central California. I would go to work, Terri and Nathan would stay home. Other than the Delfin's, we knew nobody in town. Though in God's will, those days were, yet, somewhat difficult.

We visited a couple of churches in the area checking things out and wondering what exactly the Lord wanted us to do. In my mind the desire to preach was stronger than ever. After a few months, I decided that I would start my own church. The apartment complex had a banquet room that we could use for services.

Trying to do the right thing, I called the pastor of the only other Independant Baptist Church in the town of 100,000 people, not to mention the surrounding area, which made the population to draw from about 200,000 people. He said that he would like to meet with me, and we set a date.

I asked Bro. Delfin to come with me, and he did. We walked into the pastor's office, sat down and made small talk for a little while. I then told him that I would be starting a church on the other side of town, and that in no way would I be trying to take any of his members.

He then asked me a question that kind of took me by surprise. He asked, *"By what authority are you going to start a church?"*

I thought to myself, *"By what authority? What kind of a question is that? People are dying, and going to*

Hell all over the place around here, and you ask me, by what authority?"

I then replied to him with a tone in my voice that revealed my unsureness, *"The Bible is my authority, and by the authority of the word of God I am starting a church."*

His face became very stern, his voice increased in volume, and from behind his desk he bellowed out to us, *"No sir, No sir, that is not your authority! The local church is to be your authority! You have no authority to start a church here."*

I was incredulous. My thoughts raced through my mind, *"You mean to tell me that the local church has more authority than the word of God? Nuts to you buddy!"*

I now know that the pastor was a Baptist Brider. To them, only the "true" local, independent, fundamental, Baptist church, through the pastor, has the power to baptize, send out, and insert or remove someone from the body of Jesus Christ. You could say that they are power mad, megalomaniacs, otherwise known in the Bible as Nicolaitans. (Of course I write that in Christian charity. See my book, Here Comes the Bride.) Needless to say our fellowship, or the hopes, thereof, ceased that day.

Isn't it amazing how when you get ready to do something for the Lord that you have prayed about and considered for a long time, there always seems to be someone around who will tell you that it isn't God's will, or that you are not going about it God's way?

The apartment complex we lived in had a conference room, and it was free to use for those who lived there. We arranged to use it and started Bible Believers Baptist Church.

For me it was a very exciting time. I felt like a runner who had just heard the gun sound, and it was the moment he had trained for so long, it was time to run. I was going to run as best and as hard as I could.

The Delfins started attending, Bro. Delfins sister, and a few others, one of which was a lady by the name of Laura Mushette.

Sister Mushette started coming when we knocked on her door. She lived in the apartment complex and was confined to a wheel chair. She was a quadriplegic, and, therefore, could not move her arms or legs.

Each Sunday, with her nurse's help, she would get strapped into her motorized wheel chair and come over to the meeting. Just seeing her there was a great blessing to me. I have often mused about what she will do at the rapture, when she gets her new body. What joy shall gleam from those eyes as she moves her arms and legs that for so many years had been limp and motionless.

The little church seemed to go well. Nestled in the corner of the large open banquet room, our little group of about 10 people met each Sunday. We took on some missionaries and went soul winning each Thursday evening.

On July 20, 1985, Rebekah Wahneeta McDonald was born in our small one bedroom apartment. Terri had gone to work at a local bank to pay for Rebekah's birth. All of her money, after tithe, went to the cost for Rebekah to be born. We lived on my pay. We had midwives deliver Rebekah, so she was born in our little one bedroom apartment. The one bedroom apartment was now seeming to become even smaller. We were a family of four living in a small apartment.

My job was steady, but the pay was not too good.

They did give me a work car to use, and if you counted that as an extra $1.00 an hour, then my pay was about $7.00 an hour. Financially we were always tight. Nathan for a while did not have any shoes. We would have to carry him over the hot pavement so he wouldn't burn his feet. One day we had a little extra, and we bought him some Saltwater sandles. He looked down and kept saying, *"New shoes momma, new shoes."*

By the Fall of 1985, the church was not doing good. Bro. Delfin's sister was not coming anymore. What few visitors we had were not coming.

Bro. Delfin was gone on a six month tour with the Navy. His wife, Cindy, was lonely and having a hard time with the kids. The small size of the church also wore on her, as well as us.

Looking back, I can see that the Lord was showing me that I was not in His perfect will, and that I was not a pastor, but at the time I didn't see it. All I could see was that what I had so deeply longed to do was coming to an end. My heart was heavy and my spirit low. It had come to nought, and it was time to close the church, which we did.

"Lord, what do you want me to do now? Where do you want me to go? What is your will?" My heart, and thoughts, turned towards the mountains east of Modesto, the mountains of home.

Chapter 6

TWAIN HARTE

Bible Believers Baptist Church of Modesto folded in the Fall of 1985. Most businesses fold in the Fall, and this religious one was no exception.

My prayer now was, once again, *"Lord what do you want me to do?"* I knew I was called to preach, and the burden, drive, and relentless consuming need to preach would not relinquish it's hold on me, nor did I want it to. I wanted to preach, I had to preach, it was what I was alive for, and it was what I was born to do. I was driven on, in spite of the fact that another attempt had died and was lying in the wake of my efforts like a burned out house on the side of the road, whose charred black shell is all that is left.

That is how I felt about it, though I know that "in all labor there is profit," and the souls that were saved from our efforts with that little church will meet us in Heaven one day.

New Years was upon us, and the new year was 1986.

I had graduated from Bible school in 1982, and still I was not in the ministry. This thought haunted me like a ghost.

Would I ever make it into the ministry? There were many in my class that were now either on the mission field or pastoring churches, but I was not in the ministry. My heart ached because it longed to be full-time in the ministry for my Lord and Savior Jesus Christ. But, as I looked to the future, I could see no hope, no light that it would be any time soon.

Was it a hopeless imagination, or a bad dream, to continue to follow this passion, this constant nagging at my heart to preach and to serve the Lord Jesus Christ? October, November, December were months where we had no church to attend, and were in limbo. The burden of what to do grew heavier as each fruitless day passed.

Coming home after work one day, I told Terri that I had to be alone with God and find out what He wanted me to do. I was going to go somewhere to pray, and stay there until I had an answer as to His will.

I left that evening and drove to a place in the foothills that overlooked the valley of California. It was a wide overlook beside the road that you could pull into. It was large with many parking places. I arrived there about dusk, switched to the passenger side of the little Mazda GLC, turned around and knelt. I began to confess all my sins, and to tell my Lord everything that was on my heart, as well as to ask Him for light as to His will for my life.

Ah yes! God's will! That lofty purpose for my life. To me it seemed like a cloud of vapor that kept vanishing just when I thought I had it in my grasp.

The sun set and the stars came out but I did not

notice. I prayed on, I cried on, I begged and pleaded for the Lord to give me light on His will for my life. Then I prayed something that I had not prayed before. It went something like this:

"Lord, I've never tried to live by faith before, I don't know what I am doing. Dear Lord Jesus, you can see the other sides of the mountains, and down into the valleys, but I cannot. Would you please show me what you want me to do.

Lord, I didn't call myself to preach. You called me to preach; you put this burden in me, I didn't."

I was frustrated! Inside was this burning desire to preach that I had not asked for, yet where to go?, what to do?, I had no answers. Though I knew that my Lord Jesus Christ is always right, yet a part of me wanted to lash out at the Lord for giving me this burning desire, and then thwarting my attempt at fulfilling that desire.

I prayed on seeking an answer from the Lord. Time went by as I sought the Lord Jesus Christ in earnest. Not for just myself, but I knew that my family would be best off if we were in the will of God, whatever that was. I just knew that if I was in God's perfect will all would work out, and if I wasn't in His perfect will then things would be a mess, and I would need to do whatever I had to do to get where He wanted me to be.

Then, and to this day I am still not sure why it happened, or what the Lord was trying to show me, there was a knock on my window. I had come up there to get away and seek God, and now there is a knock on my window at 10:00P.M., out almost in the middle of nowhere.

A bit concerned, I only cracked my window, as I

could not see who it was for the darkness, and asked, *"What do you want?"*

It was a young girl with a friend, about in their twenties, and their car had broken down. They wanted to know if I would help them. Wondering what the Lord was doing, I said that I would. They left their car there, and I drove them home, about an hour, which was not far from where I lived anyway.

The whole way I was wondering, *"Lord what are you doing? I am trying to get with you and these girls ask for help. Do you want me to start a church in their town?"*

I witnessed to them and they said that they were saved, yet they were a bit charismatic, though that is not uncommon in California.

It was about midnight when I dropped them off, and I then went home, still searching, still frustrated, and still with no answers.

November ran into December, and New Year's was coming soon. A church a few hours north of Modesto was having a watch night service. That is a service where you start about 7:00 P.M. and have preaching singing and eating until, or a little after midnight. It is a Christian way of bringing in the New Year. No booze, no drugs, no fornication, just a clean joyful time with God's people, singing, preaching and eating.

The pastor, Hilton Smith, had asked me to preach the watch night service, and I was the main speaker that night. My family went with me, as well as Anthony Delfin, who was back from his six-month tour.

As I write this, I wonder if this was the night, well, there is no wonder to it. This night I would get my answer to my prayer that I had prayed the night I went out to seek God's will for my life. Would I see it?

Unfortunately not!

We made it to the meeting fine, with good fellowship on the way up. It was December 31, 1985, almost three years out of Bible School, which to me seemed like an eternity. I would be preaching in the new year, which meant that I would be the last preacher, and would be preaching when midnight arrived.

The service went well with the various men from the church preaching, along with good singing, food and fellowship. At 11:30 the pastor asked me to preach. His announcement went something like this:

Light heartedly he announced, *"And now let me introduce to you evangelist Ken McDonald."* When he did, Anthony Delfin, without any prompting, and who was sitting on one side of me, turned to me and shook his head in affirmation, as if to say, *"Yes, that's right."* It was not a put on, nor was it planned. It was a spontaneous response.

Did I notice it? Yes! Did I believe it? No! Was it the Lord? Most definitely! But at the time, I still did not accept it. Me? An evangelist? I can't do that. I wasn't fighting it, I just did not believe that I could ever be an evangelist. The call was too high for me, at least in my mind, and so I would never consider that it was the Lord trying to tell me that He wanted me in evangelism. I missed the light from the Lord, and stumbled on trying to serve the Lord, trying to do right, but not in God's perfect will, and, therefore, without His blessing and help. That is a hard way to go!

That was light that night from the Lord. Direct light from Him as well as a direct answer to my long prayer up on the pull-out that night. Unfortunately, because of not accepting it then, I would end up dragging myself as well as my family through much sorrow that I did not need to go through if only I had recognized and acted on the light that God was giving me at the time.

A few months of the new year had now passed, and Spring had arrived. From the time that I had started working my job at Valley Copy Service, new accounts began to open up for the business in the mountains east of Modesto in a town called Sonora, not far from where I grew up. From one day a week to two days a week, I started driving up there for work.

With a great burden for the area, I decided to try to start a church up there. It was a dream of mine to go back home and bring the truth to the area and to the people I loved. With the work opening up in that direction, it seemed to me that the Lord was leading me in that way.

Eagerness again filled my soul. I thought to myself, and then talked it over with Terri, that maybe my friends, who were saved when I was, would be interested in a Bible study. There were a bunch of us, at one time over twenty people, who attended the Bible study before I went to Bible school. All we needed to do was to have a Bible study, get it going, and it would be a piece of cake.

So you will understand the lay out: Modesto is a city in the central valley of California, right in the middle of the state, across from San Francisco. There is much farming there as the land is very flat, because it used to be a lake, and now it was lake bottom. To the east of Modesto are the Sierra Nevada mountains. The foothills started to rise slowly about 15 miles east of Modesto. As you traveled farther and farther into the mountains, the higher and higher you would get. You would cross into Tuolumne county, and the county seat was a town called Sonora. It was nestled in the foothills at about a 1,500 to 2,000 foot elevation. Then as you traveled farther east, the hills began to rise faster, and the road became steeper. Eleven miles east of Sonora is my home town of Twain Harte. It is nestled in the mountains at just under 4,000 feet.

The weather in both places is beautiful, except Modesto, and the central valley can get fogged in during the winter months of December through March. At one point when we first arrived in Modesto and were in the apartment, it fogged in. It was during the time of the church in Modesto. The fog stayed for over 40 days, and we never got to see the sun for all those days also.

I would come home from work on Friday, which was the day I worked up in Sonora, and tell Terri that, *"It was a beautiful day today up in the mountains."* When it fogged in the valley, it was always clear and sunny up in the mountains. She looked at me depressed and said, *"You're lying, it wasn't sunny up there."* I told her it was, but she didn't believe me.

The next day was Saturday, and I told her, *"We are going to the mountains, and we will stay at Grandma T's."* We headed east and got to the foothills and started to climb into the hills. At a place called the K Arrow Ranch, the sky began to turn blue, and the sun was shining brightly. Terri's face lighted up with joy. The rolling hills were green from the early winter rain, the sky was blue, and the sun shone golden on the green hills. It had been one month since Terri had seen any sunshine.

I drove up to Twain Harte and said *"Hi"* to some family. Then prayerfully driving around I went by Russ and Lisa Hoover's house, but they were not home. I then went back down the hill to Sonora when, guess what? I saw Russ and Lisa coming out of a shop on Main Street. I stopped and said *'Hello'*. Then I asked if they would be interested in a Bible study, and they said yes. Glory to God! I cannot begin to tell you how excited I was.

I envisioned that this was the start of a new church. A Bible believeing church in the hills of California. To find Russ and Lisa the way I did had to be a sign from the Lord that He was in it. Or so I thought. And maybe He was in it. To this day, my attempt to start a church in Twain Harte seemed like it was the Lord's will at the time, but I can't say that for sure. I did know He wanted me out West, that is for sure.

I began to have Bible studies, and they went well. More and more people began to attend. Things were looking very positive about the work.

One evening back at home in Modesto, I received a call from a man I had known in Bible school. He asked if I would be interested in taking a church to pastor, and I said that I was. He then asked if I knew where Sonora was? My heart skipped a beat, and I said that I did. He said that there was an independent Baptist church up there that needed a pastor. He then gave me a phone number to call.

Oh! This was greater than I could ever imagine. I knew right where the church was, and in my mind it was more than I could ever wish for. Could it be that God was going to let me pastor the only independent Baptist church in the area. I must say, that at that time, the thought of pastoring that church was greater than all my dreams and aspirations of life. To me it was more than my heart could wish for.

I made the phone call and set up the time to candidate for the church. I told everybody at the Bible study to pray for me. That Saturday night I could not sleep. I mused on the joy of pastoring the church there in my home area where I grew up.

Sunday I was up early to get ready for the services. We were at Grandma T's house, which is at the top of a hill with the backyard being nothing but forest. Tall pine and cedar trees covered the mountains. Pine needles and oak tree leaves covered the ground. I walked out a little way into the forest with my mind on my sermon, and knelt down to pray for the meeting. I could feel that my right knee was a bit cold, but I did not want to be distracted, so I stayed in earnest prayer about the services that day. After fifteen minutes or so, I finished and stood up to go back into the house. I looked down, and I had knelt right in a pile left by a dog, probably that morning, a large dog.

In a panic, I raced into the house. It was my only suit. *"Terri, what do I do? I'm candidating for the church and my knee stinks, is wet and looks horrible."*

She took my pants, washed the knee somehow, and it turned out fine. To this day I think she worked a miracle on it.

Well, we went to church and I preached. I thought to myself, *"If they just hear me preach, it will be fine."* The service went very well with a good altar call. It looked obvious that the Lord had touched many hearts. There was just one problem. The deacon that was in charge, and that happened to also have a lot of money, was not there that day. I didn't think much about it, though, as I thought that the others who had just heard me preach would out vote him if he didn't agree, and I would be in as pastor.

We spent the day at the Ingles' house, and it was a good time of fellowship. I kept thinking to myself that I was home and fellowshipping with saved Bible believing christians. To me, it was the fulfillment of a dream. Maybe in time my mom and dad, brother and sister will get saved and start coming to church.

That evening, I preached again for the service and again it went well. I thought to myself, *"This is a done deal, the church is mine."* Some of the people even made comments that they would like me to come and pastor that church.

After the evening service, we went home. In my soul I was excited just thinking that I would be in the ministry, and on top of that, I would be in the area that I grew up in. In all of my imagination at the time, I could not imagine anything better than what appeared to be happening before my eyes.

During the ensuing week, I heard that the head deacon had notified another preacher, a Bob Jones University Graduate.

Though these thoughts are not right, yet I thought to myself, *"He probably is a lousy preacher, and he doesn't even believe the word of God."* The latter part of that thought was and is true. I thought, *"They'll see that I'm the Lord's will for them."*

After that next Sunday, I heard that he had done a good job and that they were considering him for the pastorate.

Confused, emotional, and distraught, the thought broke upon my mind that maybe I would not get the church. *"This can't be! I know it's God's will for me to pastor that church; I know it is!"*

I fasted and prayed for five days for that church. It was a hard fast as the last three days of it I had a migraine headache. The Lord was not giving me any grace for the fast, but I was determined to continue.

I then received word that the other pastor was voted in. I couldn't believe it! My hopes were dashed. So close to being in the ministry and now that evasive dream eluded my grasp once again. The ministry was like a vapor that I could not get my hands on no matter how hard I tried.

After some time, I was told that the people of the church had wanted me as their pastor, but that the head deacon had said it was the other man or nobody, and they all gave in.

The last time I was in the area, I heard that that head deacon was very unhappy and looking into starting another church because the pastor that he put in had gone to the New International Version of the Bible and compromised with other issues as well. I personally heard that preacher say in a sermon that, *"All of the Bible versions make up the word of God."*

Was it the Lord's will for me to get that church? I do not think it was God's perfect will, for I know now that I am an evangelist. But I do think that the Lord would have worked that out, as well as keeping that church a Bible believeing church.

I continued with the Bible study, but I had made one big mistake with it. I used my unsaved Grandma's house to hold Bible studies in. This was not good, for the Lord will not bless when you use a lost relative's things for His work. There may be an exception here or there, but as a rule, do not use the lost to do the work of the Lord, especially when it is relatives.

If you are paying for the services, then that is one thing. I am talking about the lost helping out with the work of the Lord. He will not bless it!

We started Bible Baptist Church of Twain Harte in the early summer of 1985. We met in a concrete block building that was used and owned by the American Legion. We rented it for twenty-five dollars per Sunday, which was very reasonable.

For the first two years, we commuted an hour and twenty minutes to the hills in order to have church. I was working full time, and we would have church on Sundays.

I remember every now and then I would be behind on my studies, and be up 'til 2 or 3 A.M. on Saturday night getting ready for Sunday. Then we would load up into our highly oxidized, red, 1980 Datsun King cab pick-up. Our truck had a camper shell on the back, so Terri would drive, Nathan would be in his car seat, and I would climb into the back of the truck. With the loud hum of the tread of the tires hitting the pavement, and with a pad under my knees, I would pray as Terri drove for over an hour to church.

The church began to grow. Without any proselytizing, a couple of the families from Grace Baptist church started coming to the services. Then others started coming and the church was getting up to about forty people. It was in a great position to take off and become established, but there was one problem.

I didn't know how to pastor. It was not just because I was young. It had to do with my call.

When the Lord calls a man to do a job, to a certain extent, that man understands what needs to be done, and how to do it. In other words, the Lord equips the man for the job He wants him to do. When a man tries to do a job that the Lord has not called him to do, he usually is confused about what to do. Or else he thinks he knows what he is doing, but there are no lasting, Biblical, results for his labors, and usually his labors are extreme.

I know a pastor who had been a missionary, and a successful one at that. In the short time that he was on the field, he had started a couple of churches. His finances were real good, and when a difficulty would arise, he had an answer of what to do about it, and usually solved the problem.

He came back to the states for deputation, to raise money to build a church building on the mission field. While on deputaion he was offered a church, and he ended up taking the church in the United States. The church has declined in every ministry since his taking it over. I heard him say many times, *"I don't know what to do."* When he was on the mission field, that didn't happen.

Since I was, and am not a pastor, I had no vision nor rapport with the people. I didn't know what to do. All I knew was preach. What's more is that the people wouldn't call me pastor. It was always Bro. Ken, or preacher, but never, or very rarely was I ever called pastor.

I don't mind being called Bro. Ken, don't get me wrong. I'm not into a power trip. But it was more than that. I noticed towards the end that people had to make an effort to call me pastor. It wasn't natural or easy for them to call me pastor. There was a subconscious understanding in the people that I wasn't a pastor.

I see that now, and I know why, but during that time, I did not know why.

The hardest time of the service for me was announcements. Announcements were a formality that I wanted to get out of the way so I could get busy with the preaching. I've watched pastors who will joke and talk to their congregations and it is just a natural thing, but it was something that I could not do. I only knew one thing and that was preach. Even to this day when I step into a pulpit all I know is preach.

Those years were very hard years. Certain days of the week I would drive in my company car, over two-hundred miles a day with stops along the way. The pay was barely enough to get by. I was making, before anything was taken out, about $800.00 a month. We usually had about ten dollars left after the bills were paid. That ten dollars would be used for shoes or other needs. The job was good, though, in one respect, it would not interfere with the ministry. I had the weekends off, as well as the evenings.

While at Bible school, we had been taught that it would be hard. We heard stories of hardship from other pastors, evangelists, and missionaries, so it was to be expected. Something else that I had never had was a real pastor. I had never been in a church with a personal pastor, so I really did not, nor had not, seen or been around a solid healthy church.

The Bible school church was great, and the men were there when you needed them, but it is not the same as a smaller, local church. That smaller, local church was something that I had no idea of what it was like, so there were many rough edges to Bible Baptist Church of Twain Harte.

We had been driving up to the mountains on Fridays after I got off work, and we would stay at my lost Grandma's house every weekend. This was completely alright with her, and she was gone from the house half of the year down in her winter house, so we had it to ourselves. But it was a lost relative, and the Lord did not bless any of this, although at the time I did not see it.

We loved being up in the mountains, though, and

we all looked forward to the weekends to get out of the city.

One weekend, as we were up in Twain Harte, my Grandma offered to purchase for us a lot to put a house on. I had not asked her for help, nor would I. She had just offered it to us, and it seemed like there were no strings attached. There were no clauses seen or unseen to which would have led me to decline the offer. It seemed right.

(Remember this, if you want God's blessing, don't use lost relatives, no matter how generous they may be.)

Could this be the Lord? I wondered, turned it over in my mind, and Terri and I talked it over. The thought excited us, as you can imagine. We had never had a house of our own, and still this was only a lot with no house on it. We had no money and were only getting by each week, but to us it was a start.

Thinking that the Lord had led us up there to start the church, it seemed possible that the Lord was using Grandma T to help us get on our feet. (Don't use lost relatives!) So, we started looking for a lot.

Then, not long after this offer from my Grandma, some friends Terri had known as a little girl when her dad was stationed in Japan in the Navy called us up out of the blue and offered to loan us the money to build a house. We had not asked for this loan, it was again unsolicited and seemed like, it too, had no strings attached.

We were so excited. To us it looked like God was going to work it out to have a house of our own. My dreams were coming true. To live in the mountains, preach the gospel, and win those people to the Lord. I had no other desire than that.

We located a nice lot, up in the mountains with a beautiful big oak tree on it, along with some other trees. About a third of an acre, on a corner, and level, which is rare in the mountains.

I signed the paper, and the proceedings started for the purchase. Everything was going very smoothly, until something happened that should have told me to stop.

The deadline was coming due for payment to be made on the property, yet there was no movement at all from my Grandma. I did not want to bring the subject up, after all, she had offered, I had taken her at her word. She had not said anything, nor had she inquired as to how things were progressing. It put me in a very uneasy situation.

It was getting close to the deadline for payment, so I went over to her house; she was sitting in the living room all by herself. I made small talk and mentioned a few things about the property, but she kind of ignored me. What was I to do? She had offered to pay for the property but my name was on the agreement.

My wife and kids had been through so much, and we all were so eager to have a house of our own. Along with this was the desire to have a church there in the mountains, and it was doing well at the time. It all looked right.

She continued to ignore me, so I opened my mouth and asked. That was my other big mistake. Other than using lost relatives, I never should have asked, but I did.

At the time I thought, *"Lord what is going on?"* And I sensed that maybe the Lord wasn't in this. I thought to myself, *"No, no we have come too far to turn back. Terri and the kids are so excited. It's just the devil trying to stop me from establishing a Bible believing Church up here in these mountains."* So I went ahead and asked for the money, and she paid for the property.

It was here, about two years into Bible Baptist Church of Twain Harte, that the ministry began to slide. If there was ever any blessing on the work, once we used the lost to help us, that blessing ceased. (Don't use the lost in the work of the Lord.)

Once the property was paid for, then we had to work out the loan from Terri's friends. They were an older couple that obviously had plenty of money. They had known Terri from when she was a little girl. She was precious to them. And they wanted to "help us" get into the house.

We witnessed to them, as we did to all of our relatives, but they were not open to the gospel.

As with the property, so now with this private loan. We were getting entangled with the lost. It was a web, a snare, that I naively fell right into.

The deal went something like this. We will loan you the money, and your payments will make us more money than we can make from a bank. There was one more thing about the deal and to this day I'm not sure what it was, but in the deal, we had to lie a little bit about the payments to them. It was one of those things where it was not a direct lie, but it certainly wasn't the truth either.

This fine print was slipped in at the end, and I should have stopped all transactions right then and there, regardless of the cost, but I didn't. The buck stops here, and I was the one who had the final say-so, but I let it go through.

I looked at my wife who had gone through so much, and she was not complaining or nagging. My kids had been hauled to and fro, from the valley to the mountains, for two years. I was worn out from the driving back and forth. These things weighed heavily on me, but that still does not make what I did right. It was not the truth, and God's blessing, if ever at all in our labors, was now removed completely.

Things began to go from bad to worse.

On one side of the property was a house inhabited by a very obnoxious man. When our house began to be built, he went berserk. Yelling, loud music, and doing anything he could to be a pest.

After the house was first framed, I went by to see it and the floor plan had been placed backwards from the way we wanted it to be built; it was too late to change it. I went to the builder, and he showed me how I had drawn it, and he had built it right, but it was not how we wanted it. My fault again!

I tried to be friendly with the neighbor, but he was completely confrontational. He then would crank up his heavy Rock music and spin his tires making dust fly all over the place.

Across the road, the another neighbor started giving us a bad time also. He shot our dog with a pellet gun and would yell across our yard to the other neighbor. Our dream home was becoming a nightmare.

When you are out of the will of God, you lose your power, spiritually as well as temporally. No matter what I did to correct the situation, it wouldn't work. When I called the cops, he would outsmart the cops. Our house was becoming a prison, or so it seemed.

A year after getting into our house the walls began sinking, and the builder had to come out and jack them up. The floor would break if I jumped up and down on it. You could hear the plywood crack.

About this time, one of my main men in the church was becoming more and more rebellious. I was trying to get the people out soul winning, and he would fight me the whole way. He ended up leaving the church, which was a big blow to me. We had been friends when we were lost, and he had been instrumental in my getting saved. Terri and his wife were close also.

As I look back on this, I can understand why he left. I am not a pastor, but he had also known me when I was lost, and a prophet hath no honor in his own country.

Then another family found out their fifteen year old daughter had been fornicating with boys, and not long after that her father was arrested for child molestation.

When he was released from jail, I tried to help him, though I should have kicked him out of church because he had lied to me about it and never repented. His presence hurt the church, as well as my lack of rebuke to him. My lack of rebuke hurt the church more than anything.

Another family had a young man who was going out drinking and messing around with girls. It was all I could take, so I preached very hard at him one Sunday morning and my only other good family got offended and left. I told them I was not preaching at them, but it was too late, they were offended and left.

During the five years that the church lasted in Twain Harte, we had four revivals. It was these revivals that taught me some of the greatest lessons that I ever learned in my attempt at being a pastor. Lessons that I would be able to use in my service for the Lord in years to come, because they taught me what not to do.

The first revival was with a family that sang and the father preached. All in all they were a blessing. I tried to have them park at Grandma T's, and it was an absolute mess. (Don't use lost relatives!!!) Their trailer almost got stuck, and they ended up breaking a lamp in the house.

I had offered to let them use the house, but he had more discernment than I, and after a day, he said that he did not think that the Lord wanted them to use the house. He could see it, though I did not.

Not long after, he moved the trailer down by the church; smart man.

One service, though, greatly hindered me as the pastor. I had this family coming to church, as well as the revival meetings, and they would always arrive late. They appeared spiritual, but there was a subtle rebellion in them. More and more they would be late. It got to the point where we would be waiting to start the services until they arrived. I did not like this and started the services without them. We sang a few songs, I gave announcements as usual, and I turned the service over to the evangelist intending for them to sing as a family, and then for him to preach. What he did really undermined me.

The "late family" was just arriving when I turned the service over to the evangelist. He got up and said, *"Lets sing a few more"*, and proceeded to lead the church in a few more songs instead of having his family sing.

He entered the pulpit and then proceeded to say that his pastor will have the people sing until they are ready for preaching, implying that I was doing it wrong. He then pointed out the family that had been rebellious and said, "They just got here and didn't even have time to sing the songs and get ready for the preaching." He rebuked me in front of my people and helped that family in their rebellion.

What he did that night hurt me. I don't mean my feelings, and let's go cry about it. But it hurt me in that ministry; he did not help me that night at all. *"Confidence in an unfaithful man in time of trouble is like a broken tooth, and a foot out of joint."* Prov. 25:19 I could sense that family rearing up in confidence against me, as well as the rest of the church losing some more confidence in my leadership as pastor.

Looking back it was one of many events that the Lord was using to try to show me that I was not a pastor, and that it was time to get out of there. But for me it was a lesson to help me as an evangelist. When I come into a church and see the pastor do something that looks odd, I realize that I don't see the whole picture. The pastor knows things that I don't and does things for reasons that I am not aware of. It is not for me to determine if he is right or wrong, and it is wrong for me to get up in his pulpit and attempt to correct the pastor in front of his people.

Though it was painful at the time, the lesson I learned that night was instilled deep within me, and I believe helped me as an evangelist. Since then I have been in many pulpits around the country, and some in other countries. I have seen pastors do many things that cause me to wonder why does he do that? But what I see with my eyes in a church, I try not to let influence what comes out of my mouth. For what I see with my eyes is rarely, if ever, a clear testimony of what is truly going on in the church. I try to look spiritually at the work, and remember that I am there to help them and be a blessing. That is not to say that I don't rebuke, for I do from the word of God. It is the word of God that will bring the rebuke without me trying to aim it.

Our second revival went well, and the man did a good job. He was used by the Lord to be a help to us.

Then we had a third revival about four years into the church. By way of testimony of the brethren, I heard that this evangelist was, *"a great man of God that will stir up your people for the Lord."*

"Well, this is exactly what I need. Sure, I'll have him in." I went in halves with another church to fly him out for a meeting. We were to drive halfway between our churches, and I would pick him up. It's just that the pastor of the other church went about one quarter of the way. It was very one sided. By now things were going so bad, that I was getting used to things not going my way.

Arriving back home, I was going to have him stay with us since our church didn't have much money, and I wanted to give him a good offering. When he found out that he was staying in our home and that during the day my wife and children would be there, he told me that it wasn't going to work, and that he needed his own place to stay.

I knew it wasn't good to have him stay in our home, but things were so tight financially that I didn't know what else to do. The Lord was very merciful, though, as I found out later that this evangelist was having affairs with women all around the country.

I called my treasurer, and we decided to put him up in a motel. Motels around there are not cheap as it is a tourist area.

He then asked if someone would iron his shirts. My wife ended up doing it as nobody else in our fifteen member church would do it.

He then asked if he could borrow a vehicle to get

around in, and I loaned him my Datsun truck, about which he complained of its size and smell. I used it to get wood in.

He then complained about the meals that were provided. They weren't what he wanted.

The Lord did not move in the services at all. One night we had a visitor who was a decent looking lady. In his preaching he looked at her in a certain way, and I heard her gasp, though at the time I did not know why. I know now.

His attitude stunk, for you could tell that he thought the church was too small for him, and his offering would not be large enough.

By now, four years into this work and I needed some help. I had hoped and prayed that this revival meeting would be a great help to us. After all, the last one was. But this one hurt. It was another broken tooth, and foot out of joint. By the time the meeting was over, the small church had spent over $1000.00 on the meeting, and was left in worse shape than before the meeting started.

That meeting put an indelible mark in my heart and mind of what not to do, and how not to be an evangelist. After finding out of his affairs with various women, it taught me that you can never be too careful in the ministry. Do all you can to avoid situations that would cause, or enable temptations. It was one of the reasons why I decided to bring my entire family from the start in evangelism.

There was one thing that he was right on, though. When he was getting ready to leave, he looked at me and said that I needed to get out of there. I was not a pastor, and that I needed to go work in an established church for a while. When he told me this, I immediately thought that it was the devil trying to discourage me. I was mad when I heard him tell me this, and decided that I would be glad when he was gone. How deceived I was! I was convinced that I was in God's will doing what he wanted me to do, and, yet, I was not.

When that evangelist left, I felt like I had been kicked in the stomach.

Time went on and the church grew smaller and smaller. Five, six, seven years out of Bible school, and I am not in the ministry full-time. Will I ever be in the ministry? More and more it seemed like a fleeting dream.

There are certain nightmares in a person's life that wake them out of a deep sleep at night as fear grips his heart as the memory of the event comes to mind. Satan brings these things back to mind also to wear us down. So to give another example of the battle we were in, I will add the following story.

We had made a casual aquaintance of a family in the area. They were a young family with two children, an older boy and younger girl about the same age as our Nathan and Rebekah, so it worked out well for the children to play together. We had also hoped the family would start coming to church.

One day Mrs. Lane asked if Terri would watch her children that day, and Terri said that she would be glad to. I went to work that morning, and not long after, Chris dropped her children off with Terri. It would be a day Terri would love to forget.

It was about midmorning on a very nice mountain day. The air was just right, the breeze was cool, and it was a perfect day for a hike. A day to get the kids outside and see a little of the countryside.

Just down the road from our house was a trail that

led out to the Crystal Falls. Terri had never seen the falls, and neither had the Lane children, so they decided to go on a hike. Having only heard of the trail there was a curiosity to go explore it.

About a quarter of a mile down the road, sure enough, was the trail, which appeared to be well traveled. It was beautiful as it wound through the tall ponderosa pine trees, incense cedars, and black oak trees. The blue jays squawked in the trees, and a squirrel chatterred a warning as they walked under the tree.

Our two dogs, Chauchie and Tetian ran ahead. The boys, Nathan and Shawn, ran ahead of Terri and the girls, getting a little bit out of sight from Terri which concerned her. Yelling to the boys to come back, she heard no answer. Rounding a corner of the trail with a quickened step of concern, she saw the Lane boy just getting up as he had slipped on the slick, mossy rock over which the small stream flowed. His knee was a little hurt, but he was alright.

It must have been an angel which guided him to fall down, as he was a boy who knew no fear, and would recklessly try anything.

Nathan looked confused and worried as Terri rounded the corner of the path and saw them both. Ahead of her was a beautiful view of the valley below, but it was obvious that they were up on the edge of a high ridge. A ridge over which the water fell about 1,000 feet to the valley below.

The granite ridge sloped slowly over, so that it was very easy to end up realizing the danger you were in too late and then falling to your death.

I had a girl in my high school class, Lisa Johnson, who died going over the falls. I knew of the danger, but Terri and the kids did not.

As Terri got closer she yelled to the boys, *"STOP. DON'T GO ANY CLOSER!"*

Then Nathan with a fearful concern said to her that Chauchie and Tetian went over the side. He watched them go over.

Going closer to the deceitful edge, Terri walked along the top of it, trying to figure out where they might have gone to, not knowing the danger she was putting herself in. She was right on the rounded precipice that fell to the valley below.

She looked and called for the dogs, but there was no answer. Nathan said he thought that he heard them bark so they listened and called, but could not hear anything.

Suddenly, realizing her danger, she got back from the edge, told the kids that the hike was over and started for home.

Rebekah asked, *"But what about Chauchie and Tetian?"* Tears began to fill the eyes of Terri, Nathan and Rebekah. The dogs were gone, they went over the edge and were gone.

Terri, beginning to realize what had just happened, began to cry knowing that Shawn, the boy, had almost gone over the falls. A boy she was supposed to take care of had almost died. If it had not been for him falling, he would have gone over. It was only the grace of God that had saved that young boy, and Terri could see it all very plainly now.

That afternoon, I arrived home to find Terri, Nathan and Rebekah crying. When the Lanes came to pick up their kids, she could not stop crying thinking how close their boy had come to falling over the edge of those falls.

That evening we drove down to the bottom of the falls and looked for the bodies of our two dogs, but we could not find anything. The bodies were not there. That seemed so strange, where were the bodies?

The next day, I believe it was Saturday, we drove back down to the bottom of the falls. After walking around, I then began to climb up the forested, steep, mountainside, which was beside the sheer granite falls. Three-fourths of the way up, I looked over to a clump of grass and willow bushes growing out of the almost verticle side of the granite, and there were our two dogs. They had spent the night there.

I thought to myself, *"Now what do I do? My dogs are stranded on the middle of Crystal Falls."* Since the Mountain Rescue team would not help us, we had to do it ourselves.

After going home and getting some long rope that I had, I went back to the falls. I had also called Skip, a young athletic man in the church to come help, and he came right away.

On the edge of the falls he anchored himself with his feet against a large outcropping rock, and I tied the rope around my waist in a Swiss seat. Slowly climbing down to the level of the dogs, I came to the end of the rope. I was hanging over the edge with no foot holds, 700 feet of air below me, two dumb dogs to the left of me, and a young man holding the rope above me.

I started to swing like a pendulum on a clock, over to the island and finally made it. Picking up one of those "dumb" dogs that I was risking my life for, I swung back across to the other side and dropped it off where there were trees growing, and it was not sheer, smooth, rock face. Then I swung back for the other dog.

In the middle of the swing, with my body flat against the verticle rock I looked down and then up. All my trust was in that rope. If that rope broke I was dead.

I thought of Jesus Christ and how all my trust is in Him to get me to Heaven. The reality of trust was implanted in my mind in a real way that day. I also thought of how crazy I was to risk my life for these two dumb dogs.

Well, I rescued the other one, and the day ended with no one getting hurt, but it would be a memory that would haunt Terri for many years, and wake her up at night in a cold sweat realizing how close the tragedy had been.

It was just another short episode of trouble that seemed to plague us more and more the longer we labored and worked to establish a Bible believing church there in the mountains.

In my mind I was perplexed at the amount of opposition we were encountering. Battle after battle, trouble upon trouble, I would pray, *"Lord, help! What is the matter? What is going on?"* All I knew was, *"Press on."*

A missionary came by and we took him on for support. As he left he was burdened for our little work. He had a son-in-law who was just out of Bible school and was looking for something to do. He told him of our need for help. Meaning well, he urged him to come and help us.

The young man gave me a call, and we set it up for him to come and see if it would be the Lord's will for him and his new family to come to the mountains and help us.

A couple of months later, he came up to see the work. I remember praying with him and the remaining men of my church on a Wednesday night service which was held at my house. It was during that prayer time that he seemed to decide to come up and help us. It was to be a nightmare, and the beginning of the end for this work in Twain Harte, though at the time I couldn't have been more excited about some "trained" help in this ministry.

We were about four years into this church, and six years out of Bible school. Our brand new house had a one inch crack between the center wall and the ceiling, and the floor was breaking under me if I jumped on it.

My neighbor was making our lives miserable with loud music and anything he could do to annoy us. I tried talking to him, calling the cops, and whatever else I could think of. I ended up putting up a fence to separate our yards. But with no money to buy the materials, I went out into the forest and cut down the trees, ripped them with a chain-saw, and hand peeled the bark off of them. I hand dug the holes for the posts, mixed the cement and built the fence from scratch. He also would shoot his gun out the window at night if dogs in the neighborhood were barking.

My morale was low, though I plodded on day after day. I did not think of leaving. Twain Harte was what I thought to be God's will for my life. I believed that I was in God's perfect will. How could I leave and quit on my Lord Jesus Christ? That was out of the question. The only way out was through.

But I had help on the way which gave me some encouragement. 2Cor. 7:6 *Nevertheless God, that comforteth those that are cast down, comforted us by the coming of Titus.* This verse seemed so appropriate for the situation. Finally I would have some help in this ministry. I thought to myself, *"The Lord has looked on us, and sent some help."*

When Brian and his family arrived, I was excited. Willing to help him get on his feet, I let him stay with us. One early Saturday morning, as we were still in bed, I heard a thud and our whole three bedroom house shook. Springing out of bed with wonder, I went to see what happened?

We had bought a kit metal building from Sears for the church to store things in, and it was still in it's unopened box waiting to be assembled. It was leaning against the front roadside of our house. The house was slightly lower than the road. Brian's borrowed van was parked up on the road. The parking brake on the van let go, and his van ran into the box against our house. Praise the Lord the box was there as it protected our house. The metal building was damaged, and that signaled the start of my new helper in this ministry.

Financially he was in a mess, as the van was borrowed. Basically he had no vehicle, no money, no job, and a wife and newborn baby boy. Now, they were living in my house. I thought to myself, *"I don't need this."*

The owner of the van came about a month later and took the van away. So now he really did not have a vehicle. I let him use my Datsun truck which, when I finally got it back, was never to be the same again.

He ended up getting a job in our local hardware store and was a lousy testimony, as he was lazy, and would make excuses as to why he needed to get out of work. In a small town like Twain Harte is, it was not helping our church's testimony at all.

We finally got him a house to live in, and he now had a job. At church some of my members were starting to gravitate to him against me. But, by this time, I really did not care. One evening he asked me if he could come and talk to me, which I agreed to. He pointed out my failures and so on. By this time I was so tired that I offered the church to him. I said that if he thought he could do better then he could have it. But that did not register with him, or he did not let it appear that it did, for he did not take it.

It was not long after, that he and I had a falling out. After writing him a letter which asked him to leave, he came over to my house, and we got in a very heated exchange. It was very unchristian and ugly. We were yelling at each other for all the neighborhood to hear. I think it was on a Saturday afternoon. By this time my morale was gone. I was spiritually drained, and my hope of being in the ministry full-time now appeared farther away than it ever had appeared before.

With the argument finally over, I turned and walked back into my house. Then, all of a sudden, our two dogs started to fight in our backyard. It was a vicious dog fight. I ran through the house to the sliding glass door, opened it and ran down the stairs to the water hose. Turning it on, I sprayed the dogs until they stopped fighting.

As they stopped I turned the water off, and this whole time from the fight with Brian to the dog fight, my ornery neighbor had been listening. When the dogs ended fighting, he then turned his garage stereo up full blast with heavy metal music that filled the neighborhood.

I felt like a punching bag that was getting hit from every side. I went into the house and lay down on the living room floor, dazed, exhausted, troubled and discouraged. *"Lord, what is going on?" "Why is all this happening?"*

It was a very dark time in my life, as well as for Terri, Nathan and Rebekah. It was a battle, a fight like I had never been in before. It was a hard time, and I did not know how I was going to make it, but all I knew was that I had to go on. I thought to myself, "The Lord blesses faithfulness. I need to be faithful."

By now the church had dwindled to ten or less. I had one new family coming. They were a blessing, as they had a good spirit and would help wherever they could. The others in the church resented this since now there was a family behind our efforts.

It had now been five years for the church, and seven years out of Bible school, being the summer of 1988. I had asked an evangelist to come in for a meeting. He was a well known evangelist, and I thought, *"Who am I to have him in?"* But I figured we needed help; he was an evangelist, that is his job, and so I asked him for a meeting. He said that it was an answer to his prayers for guidance on whether or not to come out west for meetings.

The attitude in the church was now poor. Resentment towards my faithful family permeated the services, hindering any moving of the Spirit of God. The family that had come to help me was now gone, though still in the area and in contact with at least one of the families.

Finally, the time came for the meeting. We put out flyers and advertised as best as we could. I met them at the center of town and led them to the parking lot of the American Legion Hall. We got to the hall, and needing something out of our shed, I opened the door and found a note by the one family that was against us. They had now officially left the church, and the same day, my one young man told me that he would not be coming back. I had one family left and that was it.

It had now been five long arduous years, and I had one family to show for it. It was also the start of a revival, but would there even be a revival? Would there be any meetings at all?

The evangelist was a great blessing to me. His name is Dr. Sam Gipp, and he ministered and preached just like there were 100 people there. That meant a lot to me, since I remembered the evangelist before him that had an attitude that the church was too small.

During the week it appeared that the church would not go on. It seemed likely that it was over, but in my heart I did not want to quit. *"Let's go on!"* I thought. *"I still have one good family. Maybe the Lord will bless now!"*

I went to Dr. Gipp and said, *"But I don't want to quit."* I will never forget his response. Without hesitation he laughed out loud and said, *"And stay for one family? There is nothing here to stay for."*

I'll admit that his response jabbed me; it hurt, and I did not want to receive it. But, somehow I knew he was right. After all the dreams, after all the hopes and prayers, it was time to quit, close up shop, and head down the road.

The meeting ended on Friday, and the following Sunday the one faithful family and my family showed up for church. They knew it was over, but it was one of the hardest things I have ever done. I had to quit that little church.

That Sunday we started just like any other Sunday. We opened with prayer and started singing some hymns. While we sang the hymns, John was looking at me with this slight grin on his face that seemed to say, *"Ken are you going to end it? You know it's over."* We sang about four hymns, and I knew that I had to announce that it was over. I can't tell you how hard it was.

I then announced that this would be the last service of Bible Baptist Church, and the church closed that day.

Was it pride? Probably! I didn't want to quit. It meant that I had to admit failure. I had to face the fact that I was not in the ministry anymore. I was not in the ministry after seven years out of Bible school. The work I had so greatly labored for, as well as my wife and kids, was now over. It had failed, and I had to accept the truth that I had failed.

My call to preach, my aspiration of being in the ministry was to me, now a fleeting dream that seemed to vanish like a vapor never to be seen again. My purpose for living, to serve the Lord Jesus Christ, and to preach, was now vanquished. A dread and fear crept over me.

A realization was now before me. If my spiritual job was over in Twain Harte, then there was no reason to stay. With no SPIRITUAL reason to live there, then we would have to sell our house and move. Our first house that we had built, except it was built with money from lost people, and now, though not then, I know that it did not have God's blessing. (DON'T use lost people or relatives.)

I looked upon selling and moving out of the house with a certain eagerness. It was not a pleasant thought for Terri. This was her home, her first home. We had many good memories there in spite of the neighbor and problems.

Memories of the fire going in the wood stove as the snow fell outside. We were all warm and cozy in our little mountain house. Memories of a vegetable garden with tomatoes, squash, peppers etc. grown fresh for the eating. Memories of the smell of fresh cut fire wood filling the air as we stacked it in the yard, waiting for that cool crisp air in the Fall. Memories of Christmas, and holiday meals with friends and family over. It was a place of security to her. A kitchen, bedrooms, and our own bathrooms.

When I mentioned we would be leaving the area, I could see a shudder of concern go through her. She did not want to go. She was tired, as we all were. But God gave me a jewel of a wife, and she would follow me if I said we had to move.

With no spiritual reason to be there, I knew, yes, it was time to move.

Chapter 7

MONTANA

We had been in one place for five years. It was the longest time in our marriage that we had been in one single place. Now, with no spiritual reason to stay, it was time to leave.

To the flesh, the mountains called and seemed to say, *"Stay a while longer. Don't be too hasty."*

Inside I knew that if I did not act fairly quickly then it would only become harder to leave, and eventually we would not go anywhere. I was not in a panic, but I was determined that we needed to get out of there.

During our last revival, Dr. Gipp had told me about a preacher in Montana that needed some help. He told me that he had talked to him on the phone, but had not been able to go by and preach for him, so he had never actually seen the work there.

I was thinking that we needed to go somewhere and let the dust settle, get our wits about us, so to speak, and regroup for the service of the Lord Jesus Christ.

We were in no shape to do spiritual battle in the service of the Lord, we needed to heal a bit.

We were like a mother who had been in labor for many days, strength gone, exhausted, only to give birth to a dead baby. She needs time to heal, rest and get back on her feet. We too, needed to heal, rest, and get back on our spiritual feet.

I called the pastor in Montana two or three times, not sure if it was the Lord's will to move up there or not. We had good conversation, and the picture he painted was a good one. I prayed about it, and considered it, but I wanted to go and check it out before I moved my family all that way.

In the mean time, Terri and I painted the inside of our house, and got it ready to sell. We then put it on the market, and the house sold in two weeks.

As I look back on it now, I can see that it was the Lord saying to us, *"Get out of there!"* The house sold so fast that the final day to move out, the new owners were on our doorstep waiting so they could move in, and paid us an extra one hundred dollars to move out as fast as we did. The Lord was pushing us out of there.

The selling price was good, and we cleared $47,000.00 dollars when it was all done. After tithe, we had $38,000.00 in the bank. With the tithe we helped get a book printed that another evangelist had written, and the Lord used it in a major way in the Philippines, praise the Lord.

Something that I have not mentioned is the packing, moving and the amount of work it takes to pack and move. We were already beat and tired from the five years of ministry. Now we had to pack everything into boxes and move it to storage. We used rolls of tape and

U-haul boxes since they would stack right. Truckload after truckload went to storage, and there were yard sales and flea markets for the things that we wanted to get rid of.

I think it was hardest on my son Nathan. He loved his bedroom. His dog would sleep on his bed. He had airplanes and other projects young boys have. It was his place, and now he had to give it up.

No, it is not much compared to what Jesus Christ gave up for you and me, so that we could be saved, born again, and go to Heaven. But here, we are talking about a seven year old boy who had no idea of all the difficulties that were going on. All he could see was that he was losing his clean bed, and his secure bedroom. His stable world was being turned upside down.

We were out of the house, and into another bad mistake. With her permission, I moved back into Grandma T's until we knew where we were going. (DON'T USE LOST PEOPLE in your work for the Lord.)

Within a few weeks I decided that we would go up to Montana and help this pastor, but it still bothered me that I was not able to go up there and check it out. I could not go because I was not able to get away from my job. There was no one to fill in for me. I suggested that Terri could go up and check it out for me, but she did not like that idea as she was a woman and didn't want the responsibility of the decision, which I could understand.

My father said to me to be careful as anyone would want free help. *"Son, you had better be careful. He is just getting free help, and you are going all that way and not getting anything in return."* I listened, but thought that he didn't understand how important the work experience would be. He wasn't saved, so his advice was purely carnal advice, and I was looking at things spiritually, so he wouldn't understand, at least this is what I thought. The children of this world are wiser than the children of light.

During these months of transition, the Lord was working in my life, giving me light as to His will for my life. I noticed it a little, but I did not believe it.

At work there was a man that would come and do maintenence on my copy machine; his name was Nick. I found out that he was saved and went to a Baptist church. I then found out from him that he believed that the King James Bible was the word of God, and his church did also. This got my attention, and since we did not have a church to go to, we drove the hour and then some, in order to go to his church.

The pastor was an older man and was in a spiritually deep valley. His wife was dying from cancer. She was home at times, and then he would have to take her back to the hospital. During this time, he asked me if I would preach for him.

Meeting in a real estate office, the room was packed with about thirty-five people. The desks were moved to the side, and some folding chairs were set up in the small office. I preached and the service went very well. Two of Nick's boys, about eleven and thirteen years old, came forward and got saved. Others made their way to the small altar up front. It was a very good service.

I ended up preaching there three or four times, and all of the services went very well. It was a great encouragement to Terri and I. Even my faithful family from the Twain Harte church came over, and they enjoyed it too.

A thought entered my mind. Maybe the Lord wants me to be an evangelist. Could that be God's will for my life?

Ah yes! God's will. That lofty purpose for me. The reason I was alive. The duty of all on this earth, to find God's will for their life and then do it. There is no higher aspiration, there is no greater privilege than to do what your Creator wants you to do. It was His will, and the burning desire to fulfill His will for my life that drove me on, in spite of the trials and heartaches.

Could it be that the Lord Jesus Christ wants me to be an evangelist? The thought permeated my mind.

Still low in spirit, still confused as to what to do, wondering about evangelism, I went by to visit my Grandma McDonald. She was the christian anchor of our family. Everyone knew she was a christian, and I would go by, visit her and pray with her.

As I sat by her bedside, for she was confined to her bed, I looked over at her. She was down to about ninety pounds. Her delicate high, squeaky voice would reach my ears. We would talk about the Lord Jesus Christ, and she would ask how I was doing?

I told her that the church had closed and then in the course of the conversation I said to her, *"Grandma, I think that maybe the Lord wants me to be an evangelist."* Though in my mind it seemed to me to be a preposterous idea.

Her answer nearly knocked me on the floor. Without hesitation she looked at me and said in her sweet high squeaky voice, *"I always thought that's what you should do."*

Stunned, I replied, *"YYYou did?"*

"Yes, I always thought that you should be an evangelist,

and I never had any real peace about you starting the church in Twain Harte." Whatever we talked about after that I do not remember. Here was encouragement for evangelism, and I was so scared of the call I didn't know what to do.

Looking back you see things that you don't see when you are going through them. I noticed that Grandma never had peace about me and the church in Twain Harte. When I would go and see her she would ask about the church, and I would tell her that it wasn't going well. She could tell that things weren't right. But even from the start of the church, there seemed to be a hesitation in her about me and the church.

I completely did not expect this answer. It shook me that day. Is this the Lord? What am I to do? Where do I go from here? There was a fear that gripped me as the thought of evangelism confronted me.

There again was another bit of light from the Lord about God's will for my life.

We went by to see the lady who had been our church pianist. Even though she had also left the church, we were still friends. She was up in years and her son and his wife were in the church early on.

The news that I was kicking around the notion of being an evangelist had reached her. She had mentioned it to her daughter in law. Immediately her daughter in law responded, "That's what I always thought he should do."

Again, this shocked me. Evangelism? Me, an evangelist? I did not know what to think, or how to respond. And to think that she had been thinking this for some time, it was not some spur of the moment thought, but something that she had noticed long before this time.

I did not know what to do with these two rays of light. I did not even know if they were from God or not. The only thing I knew was that we had to get out of there and go somewhere to get revived, rejuvenated, and back on our feet.

With $38,000.00 in the bank there was hope that we could go somewhere and make a fresh start, buy a house, rest up, and seek the Lord's will for my life. Even though light had been given to me, I did not know if it was from the Lord or not.

I did not have a pastor to ask for advice, I was on my own. Ever since I was saved I had been to a certain extent, on my own.

With the decision finally made that we would go to Montana, I rented a U-haul truck. The truck was a mid-sized one, and in order to get all of our things in it, I had to carefully pack every square inch of it. It was not easy. There was absolutely no extra room in the cargo box, and the load was at the limit on what that truck should carry.

I write that because I can see that the difficulty that I was now encountering was due to the lack of it being God's will for us to move up to Montana. We did not have God's blessing on the move right from the start. I see that now, but I did not see that then.

Terri and Nathan rode in our little Honda Accord. Rebekah and I climbed into the U-haul. With excitement and anticipation, we set out for Missoula, Montana.

We had decided to go a different way around Sacramento when we reached there. (I write this as all of these little things, as I look back, were little flags from the Lord to show me that it wasn't His will for us to go to Montana.) Upon arriving at Sacramento, I saw that the different way around the city was not going to work, so I went the usual way. Terri was ahead of me and went the other way, and we got separated. I figured she new where I was going, that being Montana, and would catch up in a while. What I didn't realize was that she was in great distress seeing that we were no longer together.

I kept heading on the highway and in about a half hour, here she came. We pulled off, and it took a little time for her to calm down. Only three hours into our trip to Montana and already there had been some trouble. Did I notice this? No! If God wants us in Montana things like this are to be expected. Press on, don't quit, there is work to do.

As we were heading across Nevada, the truck drank fuel faster than I expected. Running on empty, I pulled up alongside of Terri and told her that I was almost out of fuel. Coasting down the hills and keeping my speed at 45mph, I limped into a fuel station just in time and filled up. *"But that was my fault,"* I thought to myself. It couldn't be the Lord showing me that He didn't want us up there. *"From now on I will fill it when it gets below a half tank."*

Not long after that, the truck started to have mechanical problems, and it swayed horribly in the winds as the load was too heavy for it. The mechanical problems were such that I could still drive the truck, but lights and gauges were not working properly. Mile after mile we drove on to our new life, our new future, and a time to heal from what we had just been through.

Missoula, Montana was our destination. The closer we got the more excited we became. Look at those mountains! Look at the rivers, and patches of snow on the mountains. It was early summertime and the scenery was beautiful. We drove into Missoula and followed our directions to where the church was. So this was Missoula. This was our new home!

I was doing fine as we drove down the streets to where the church was. We were all excited, and in a way, I was glad to be out of Twain Harte, my five year nightmare. Everything was fine until.....until I pulled into the parking lot of the church.

Have you ever bought a car, drive it home, and realized you made a big mistake? Have you ever done something and in the middle of it realized, *"I made a real big boo boo?"* That is exactly how I felt the moment I pulled into the parking lot of the church, which at the time, was being held in an empty old office building that was up for sale.

Let me explain something here. What one ministry may look like to one man who is in God's will, the same ministry will look completely different to another man who is not in God's will, or is not called to that work. The pastor of this little work is a good man and the work has grown, by the blessing of God, into a great work for God. So this is absolutely no reflection on this pastor.

I thought to myself, *"I have just sold my house, quit my job, to move up here to this? I have made a big mistake!"* That was the first thought that went through my mind. The second thought was that I wish we would have checked it out before we pulled up stakes and moved up here.

My family and I didn't need to help establish a church, we needed a church where we could heal spiritually, and get light as to God's will for our lives. I felt like I had been kicked in the stomach. I also hurt for my family whom I had brought up to this place.

They had no choice but to follow, and their leader had made a big mistake. Now they would have to suffer some more. That bothered and hurt me.

We unloaded our things into the building. I decided that we would live in the building for a while until I could figure out what to do next. We were in a big mess, and Terri and I knew it.

There was no shower or bathtub in the building, so we had to wash in a small sink with a wash cloth. Terri tried to cook on a two burner hot plate.

Just as I figured, the pastor was highly motivated and ready to go, but I was not at all. We were all exhausted and three days after getting there the pastor would walk down the hall to us while we were still in bed. Though he would not come into our rooms, he was trying to get us up. There was no consideration for us, nor was there any understanding of what condition we were in.

He started giving me things to do in the church, like empty the baptistry bucket by bucket (since there was no drain), or fill it, I can't remember which. But I didn't need things to do. I needed to get my family settled, and we all needed rest.

I never will forget one day as long as I live. We had been there about a week. After looking around the area I realized to my surprise, that the cost of living was about equal to that of California. I did not expect this. Yes, we had money, but I was not ready to put it all down on something, especially without a job. We would have to stay in that run down building for awhile.

My son Nathan was confused about it all. He remembered his bedroom and his clean comfortable bed. He had heard that we would get another house when we got to Montana, and he was longing to have a bedroom again.

I was in the room with all of our boxed things stacked up and he walked up to me, seven years old, and asked, *"So dad, when are we moving?"* Perplexed, I asked him, *"What do you mean?"* He replied, *"When are we going to get a house of our own?"* I looked at him and as tenderly as I new how I said, *"We're not Nate; it's going to be awhile before we can get into a house."* He broke down and cried. As he did I could see the pain on his face as the realization hit him that his bedroom was gone.

My heart went out to him, and I tried to comfort him, but I fell so far short. I had caused this pain, the responsibility was with me. He was hurting and longing for the comforts of a home, and this old building sure did not feel like home.

With the difficulties of trying to comfort my family, I then had the pastor coming into the building in the morning and giving me things that he wanted done as well as visits he wanted me to make with him that day.

I prayed and cried and cried and prayed. I didn't need this, my wife didn't need this, and my children didn't need this. What do I do? If it is not God's will for us to be here then we need to leave, but where do we go?

There was an urgency welling up in me. An urgency that I knew my family would not be able to take much more of this. They were weaker, and they were at the end of their emotional rope.

My mind raced back and forth for an answer, for light, for a door that through which I could step to find out what to do and where to go. The only place I could think of was that little church back in California in the Real Estate building.

The pastor's wife had gone home to be with the Lord. The pastor was still there, but only until they got a new pastor to take his place.

I prayed and gave him a call. *"Do you still need a man to take the church?"* He told me they did. I told him that I had made a big mistake in coming to Montana, and I would like to candidate for the church.

He told me that he thought they would vote me in if I came back, but that he could not promise me anything. I told him I would be coming back, and I would be praying that they would vote me in as pastor. Again, as in Tujunga, knowing that Montana was not the Lord's will, at least I knew that half of my decision was right.

It was an act of desperation, but I also did not know what else to do. I did not trust the counsel of the pastor where I was since he would counsel me to stay and help with the work. I knew that's what his counsel would be.

At the time, he was in a very rough situation with bills and other concerns, and he did need help, but I was not the one to help him, and I knew it. How do I tell him? I know it will discourage him, but I have no choice. I just had to do it, and I did.

I could see the discouragement on his face when I told him. It hurt him, and I hated that, but I had no choice. I had to get out of there.

We rented another truck, a Ryder, and it was larger than the one we moved up there with. We literally threw our things into it as fast as we could.

The trip back to California went smoothly with absolutely no problems. This had to be God's will, or so I thought.

Ah yes, God's will. My attempt to do God's will was at the root of all of this trouble, but I knew God's will is worth it. Besides, it wasn't His fault I was making such a mess of things. That was my own blindness and lack of faith to act on and accept the light that He had already given me.

Now we had light. In my mind I thought, *"The Lord did not want us in Montana. This door has opened in Valley Springs, CA, so this must be God's will. It must be God's will."*

Chapter 8

VALLEY SPRINGS

It had been three weeks since we left for Montana. At the time the anticipation of leaving and going to another place overcame what weariness and fatigue we all felt.

Now we were back. The trip had taken us over twenty five hundred miles up and back. It had consumed about five thousand dollars. And it had worn us down that much more.

Valley Springs is a wide spot in the road and is located in the foothills of Central California. When we arrived there, it was late June and very hot. In the day it would reach 115 degrees. It was a little over an hour from Twain Harte.

The little church had moved from the Real Estate business office to an excellent location on a main road in a mostly country area. The building they now rented was a nice three bedroom, two bath home with an attached garage to it. It had plenty of parking and had a good curbside appearance.

The Sunday arrived when I would candidate for the church. I was only a little nervous for I had preached there before, and it had always gone very well. I taught Sunday school, and then preached to the people.

Before the service, Terri and I had prayed and talked it over. We had decided that we would have to live in the church building because the cost of living around there was extremely high. We both agreed, but I was not sure of it. What would I do if they would not let us stay in the church? How could I say no after all that we have been through? Where would we go, and what would we do? So much was going through my mind.

After the morning service, the pastor led the business meeting. Terri and I were asked to wait in another room. Time went by, and then more time went by. What I thought would be a sure thing was turning into something else.

After about forty five minutes the door opened, and I was asked to come in. As I walked into the room, it was hot and stuffy. The atmosphere was tense. I stepped up in front of the people, blind to what was going on.

To me, taking that little church seemed so right. It seemed like it had to be God's will. Now there was a twist in the plans, and it was taking me by surprise.

I was now standing in front of the people, with the old pastor beside me. He said to me, *"The people have voted to take you as their pastor, if you do not live in the church."*

With all of their eyes focused on me, and this coming as a complete surprise, I did not know what to do. I had not allowed for this to happen.

My mind raced furiously trying to decide what was the right thing? What did the Lord want me to do? I did not know. Terri was in the other room mouthing to me through the open door, *"No, tell them no."* But I did not see her.

I mumbled something to myself, and then the old pastor looked at me and impatiently said, *"Do you want it, or don't you?"* I looked at him and said, *"Yes, I'll take it."*

I thought it was God's will, I honestly did. But, my oh my, what another mistake I was making.

The little church in Valley Springs had been saving, and they had $7,000.00 in the bank. Because they would not let us live in the church, they decided to rent us a house.

We looked all over the area, and the only house we could find was a nice house that rented for $750.00 a month. It was all we could find, and they willingly rented it for us to live in.

We moved all our things in. Finally, a home again! Nathan and Rebekah had a bedroom, Terri had a kitchen, and I was full-time in the ministry. We were all exhausted, but things were looking up.

The very next Wednesday evening service was very sparsely attended, but I thought nothing of it as I knew that I would have my work cut out for me. Wednesdays usually are low in attendance.

Then Sunday arrived. It had been one week since being voted in. I was prayed up and ready to go, eager to start this new ministry. Eager to preach and minister the word of God. I anticipated another good service, just like we had had in all, and I mean all of the other services.

We all loaded up and arrived early at the church to get ready for the services. Closer and closer it got to 10:00 A.M. and there were only a couple of people there. When Sunday School started there were eight people there, and four of them were the Johnsons, the faithful family that I had in Twain Harte. They were coming over to Valley Springs when they heard that I was there.

When the main 11:00 A.M. service started there were about ten people there. I wondered, "Where did all the people go?" Something was definitely wrong. Over the next ensuing weeks, the attendance stayed the same.

The attendance had gone from thirty to forty people who were enthusiastic about the church and the Lord, to eight to ten people, and four were my faithful ones from home. In one week the attendance had dropped to ten.

I visited the people who had been coming and asked if anything was wrong, and that we missed them at church. They would not give me any feedback as to why they were not there. No one would say anything to me. I was stunned with it all. I was right back in the same situation that I had been in Twain Harte. A small church that wasn't making it, except this time I was worn out and did not have the motivation to try to get it going.

The days were hot, too hot to get out and visit people. The church did not have the money to turn the airconditioner on. I would stay at home, which had a swamp cooler that was inexpensive to run, but it didn't cool the house all that much, though it was livable.

Tempers would flare around the house; things were just not going well. *"Lord am I in your will? God, all I want to do is your will. I have prayed, and every decision I've made I've tried to do what I thought you wanted me to do."* I would pray and pray.

I watched as the money in the savings of the church kept dropping. The church attendance was not picking up. All of July there was no sign of change in the church. Seven thousand dollars dropped to $4,000.00 and there was no sign that things would change.

Pastor Lay, the former pastor, was in and out of the area from time to time. He invited me to go with him to a Baptist Bible Fellowship meeting. I was going to meet the "Good 'Ol Boy" network. There were certain influential pastors there, and this pastor wanted me to meet them. He knew the trouble I was in, and he was trying to help me out.

We arrived at the church fellowship hall which had been set up with food and refreshments. There were many people there. Pastors and their wives as well as friends and church members. The pastors were checking me out, and I knew if I acted right and told them what they wanted to hear, I would be on easy street. They would take me on for support, and I could stay in the ministry regardless of what shape the church was in.

It was 1989, seven years since my graduating from Bible school. I had no real spiritual victories in the ministry, though I had not stopped laboring for my Lord and Savior Jesus Christ. This was the first time that I had been full-time in the ministry. Something that I had dreamed of.

Mingling around me were seasoned pastors who had connections with other pastors. Sort of a loose network of men who looked out for each other. They were seasoned in the ministry, successful, established, and comfortable in their position in life.

I was introduced to a couple of pastors, yet they

kept their distance. One of the main pastors came up to me and introduced himself to me. I forget his name, nor does it matter. He then asked me where I went to school.

I knew exactly what was going on. They had great respect for Pastor Lay, as well they should have, for he was a good man. They knew the work was having a rough time, but the kid that took the work over had not graduated from one of their "approved schools."

As a matter of fact, I had graduated from Pensacola Bible Institute, and to them I might as well had the Mark of the Beast on my forehead. Though they wanted so much to help the little church out of respect for Pastor Lay, yet they would not do it if it meant supporting a "Ruckmanite."

This main pastor was a very domineering type man and bluntly asked where I went to school. I told him that I went to Pensacola Bible Institue. He knew it was Dr. Ruckman's school. When I told him he jerked, immediately left, and I never heard from him again.

A voice seemed to whisper to me, *"You're being too hard. Give in and play their game. You can be in the ministry like you have always wanted. Compromise just a little, it won't hurt anything."* Nothin' doing on my end. Though I was worn and discouraged, I still knew that crowd wasn't right on doctrine, and the word of God, and I wasn't going to compromise just for a dollar.

I went home that day, and over the next few months I watched the church continue to slide in the wrong direction. Attendance was dropping farther, and so was the bank account.

Discouragement ran high, and my spirits were very low. After all that we had been through, it was time to take a vacation. We needed to get away, spend some time as a family. It was very needed.

I had a man fill in for me at church, and we took off to get out of the heat. We went to the northern coast of California. It was so good to get away and to be together as a family. We used money from our savings to pay for it, and we had a good time.

I tried not to let it show, though I'm sure it did, that I was troubled about the church. What was God's will for my life? Was I in His will, or was I not? It did not seem like I was in His will. What about what Grandma said to me about being an evangelist, and what about what Lisa had said about me being an evangelist? Lord, is that Your will for me? These thoughts and contemplations tortured me day and night since I did not have answers to these questions.

When the subject of evangelism would come up, Terri seemed at peace with it. She had no problems with it, but she did not want to influence me for fear she was wrong.

Four or five days into our vacation, I asked Terri what she thought about heading up to Dr. Ken Blue's church in Washington. We weren't all that far from them, maybe 500 miles. I could drive it over night. *"Okay let's go."* We loaded up and headed for Washington.

We had talked about where we would go if I quit the church, and this was the only place I knew of that was established and that I thought could be a place to sit and let the dust settle. I also wanted to make sure that I had done a survey trip before moving again. What a better chance than now for all of us to check it out.

I drove all night and upon arrival at Lynnwood, Washington, we drove by the church after getting settled into a motel. There on the marquee in front of the church was a sign stating that they were at the start of special meetings. Praise the Lord, we are going to get in on some preaching. I was excited! I had not been preached to for years.

Sunday morning we arrived at the church and attended the meetings. At the 11:00 A.M. service the evangelist began to preach. It "just so happened" that he was preaching on the subject of how he had been out of God's will for ten years. The Lord had called him to be an evangelist, and his pastor had told him that it was God's will for him to work in the Christian school at his church.

Through the message I noticed that Terri could hardly contain herself. It seemed like she was convinced that the message was for me, though she did not say that to me directly. She did not want to influence me knowing that she might be wrong, so she tried to contain herself.

By the end of the message I was broken, without her saying one thing to me.

Though the church was a large church that would seat 2,000 people, I did not care. I went forward and fell on the altar in tears. Failure upon failure had been my past. Nothing had gone right. I was exhausted from the labors, and the thought of evangelism terrified me. But there at that altar, I surrendered to the call of evangelism.

Most of the church had gone home and I was still at the altar weeping. Pastor Blue came over and put his hand on my shoulder and asked, *"Can I help you?"*

I wiped my tear-filled eyes, looked up at him and said, *"I believe God wants me to be an evangelist."*

He looked at me and replied, *"Well, maybe you had*

better talk to the evangelist."

I agreed and after wiping my eyes with a tissue, I went to the back of the church and waited for the evangelist to come and talk to me. I was broken, but had regained my composure.

He walked in and came over to me. His first words were, *"Can you make this quick, I'm hungry and want to go eat."*

It kind of took me aback so I tried to make light of it and replied, *"It won't hurt you to fast a little."*

He then shot back, *"I fast one day a week and Sunday is not it."*

Okay, we're really doing good here aren't we? So I quickly told him of my trouble in Twain Harte, and now in Valley Springs. I told him how I believed that the Lord was leading me into evangelism.

I had been praying and laboring for years to find God's will. But in less than a minute the evangelist looked at me and said, *"No, that's not God's will for you. You are just discouraged. Go back to that little church and keep going. You're just discouraged."* With that he left and had lunch.

Well, if that is his advice, then I guess that is what I should do. My thinking was that he was a successful man of God in the ministry, so I should listen to him. After all, what success did I have in the ministry? All I had was eight years of failure, therefore, my thoughts are probably wrong. This is not to feel sorry for myself, to me, it was looking at things objectively.

It is amazing to me to look back and see how quickly I had forgotten about what I had just done. I had surrendered to the call of evangelism. I believed that God was dealing with me about evangelism. But in less than five minutes that was all erased from my mind and heart.

Terri later told me that she was so frustrated when she heard what he had counseled, and that I was going to listen to him. I did not have the confidence to go on my thoughts alone. I was scared about the call to evangelism; to me it was a call that I could not do. That belief, not just a thought, was so real to me that when I was confronted with the call, I would ignore it.

Evangelist? I can't do that; it must be something else. That is how I looked at it. But, now God was bringing it into view in a way that I could not ignore.

With the Evangelist saying what he said, I was more than willing to believe him. I reasoned to myself, *"Yes, it was a foolish thought, and I am discouraged. It makes sense to me too. I don't want to go back to the church, but that must be what the Lord wants me to do. I guess that's God's will."*

It may seem like I mention God's will a lot, but I assure you I am not exaggerating. God's will for my life permeates my mind constantly. I am in a constant state of examination as to whether or not I am in His direct, perfect will.

We went back to Valley Springs, and I attempted to renew my efforts to establish that little church, but it was to no avail.

Just eight months earlier the church in Twain Harte had folded. I had watched it decline for three years, and I knew the signs. This one had all the same signs as the church in Twain Harte.

What bothered me the most was watching the church bank account drop from $7,000.00 to $4,000.00, and I knew it would continue until it was all gone. I was troubled about this. This was God's money. God's people had given it to Him for the establishment of this church, and I was watching it go.

It was this thought that caused me to make up my mind to leave. I was not going to stay and use up that money. I had absolutely no faith that the church would improve under my pastorate. I knew that it wouldn't improve if I stayed, and I had to resign and get out of there.

If I left, there might be a chance that another man could get it on it's feet.

After another month of ministering in the church, I resigned. The few people that were there didn't understand. I tried to explain, but I think they were a little hurt. For me and them, it was the right thing to do.

They ended up getting a young man who was affiliated with the Bible Baptist Fellowship. He was able to get support since he had graduated from one of their approved schools. All in all he is doing a good job, and the church is still going.

Funny thing, though. When they voted him in as pastor, they let him and his family live in the church. When I heard that, I could see the hand of God. He had not wanted me there.

Not long after resigning the church, we moved to Washington.

In five months we had moved three times. The moves covered over three thousand miles. We had completely unpacked and moved into the house there in Valley Springs. Now we had to pack it all up again.

When I pulled out some boxes, and the kids heard the tape, they started to cry. By now they knew what the sound of packing tape meant, and it was not a joyful sound!

These were hard times for us. Eight years out of Bible school and there was no sign that I would ever be in the ministry. Even the thought was not entertained in my mind anymore. I knew that we just needed to go somewhere to stay put and rest, beyond that I had no idea.

God's will for my life? Who knows? I sure didn't. We needed a good church. We needed to heal. We needed help!

Every time I thought that things could not get any worse, they got worse. Little did I know what was up ahead.

Chapter 9

WASHINGTON

Where do I go from here? To me there was only one place to go, and that was to Open Door Baptist Church in Washington state. Was it God's will to go there? I did not know for sure. By this time I did not know where to go or what to do. All I knew was that we needed to go somewhere that was established, let the dust settle, and get our lives in order as best as we could. I had been told that I needed to go sit under a man and learn some things, so that is what I did. We had taken a survey trip to Washington, and it was an established, good church, so that is where we headed.

It had now been about eight years since I had graduated from Bible school. Our first trip to Lodi, and then to Tujunga was a complete failure. They said that the Lord would never use Ken McDonald, and now I was beginning to believe them. With that thought came a great discouragement.

Modesto was a failure. Twain Harte was a failure

after five years of labor. Montana was a failure. Valley Springs was a failure. Let me just go somewhere and sit.

The last two years in Twain Harte were especially hard. Added onto them were the moves to Montana, and back to Valley Springs, and now to Washington. Our lives had been turned upside down over and over again. The money in the bank was dropping and was now around $30,000.00. Discouragement was growing in my soul, yet the call to preach would not leave me alone. It hounded me every day. I must preach, I must preach.

At times I would yell at the Lord Jesus Christ. *"You called me to preach. I didn't call myself to preach. God's will, God's will; Lord what is Your will for me? I'm trying to find Your will, but what am I doing wrong?"*

There was a part of me that wanted to lash out at God. I resented the call to preach. The hurt and bitterness that sought to grow in my heart would try to convince me that God was getting joy out of watching me flounder after putting the call to preach in me. If I would have given into those emotions, I would have ended up spiritually shipwrecked in the ocean of life.

I knew He was not that way. I knew He wanted me to find and accomplish His will more than I did. Without a doubt, it had to be my fault.

We rented yet another moving truck, packed all of our things again, and headed for Washington.

Our faithful family from the Twain Harte church had some friends that lived up by Lynnwood, Washington, and we had met them some months earlier when they came down to visit.

After contacting them for us, it was arranged for us to stay with them until we could get on our feet.

Back on the road again with another 1,000-mile move through northern California, Oregon, and then into Washington. I was pulling my Datsun pick-up behind the moving truck, and Terri was following in our Honda.

While I was driving on the highway to the east of Seattle, a man pulled up along side of me, stuck out his hand, and gave me the thumbs down, and shook his head. I didn't care, but little things like that I began to take notice of.

As I have looked back over the years of Twain Harte, Montana, and Tujunga, little things like that I could see that if I would have recognized them at the time, it would have saved my family and me a bunch of grief. By themselves they are not conclusive, but coupled with other events, they would have given me light much sooner to make a right decision.

Up to this point, there were little things in my life that also pointed towards evangelism. They were little things that in and of themselves meant little, but I did not see them, or I didn't have the faith to believe that they were from the Lord, as He tried to show me His call for my life.

It was turning into many years, about twelve, since my call to preach, and I would often look back over them. I remember my first sermon that I ever preached. It was at First Baptist in Sonora, and when I was finished a young girl came up to me and said that I reminded her of the evangelist that we had had in for a revival.

I would think about what Lisa had said, that she had thought that I should be an evangelist. I would muse on what Grandma had said, that she had always thought that I should be an evangelist. I now thought on the meetings at Valley Springs and how they went well when I was there as a visiting preacher, but when I took the church, it lost God's blessing and fell apart.

As time would go by, each one of these events in my life would have an effect on me, finally making me realize that it was the Lord's will for me to be an evangelist. But, at this point, they were only considerations to think on, not knowing if the Lord was in them or not.

We arrived at our acquaintances' house, and they were very gracious to us. They were in a country location where the houses were fairly spread out. They had a small, weather tight storage building they let us store all of our things in so we didn't need to rent a storage unit. I thought to myself, *"Thank you, Lord, for working that out for us. It looks like You are in this move."*

I was doing all I could to stop the shrinking of our savings. As I saw the savings shrink, to me, it meant that I was not providing for my family, and that I was not doing my duty to take care of them, even though I was attempting to do everything I could. *"Ye have sown much, and bring in little; ye eat, but ye have not enough; ye drink, but ye are not filled with drink; ye clothe you, but there is none warm; and he that earneth wages earneth wages to put it into a bag with holes."* Hag. 1:6 Our bag of money was leaking, and I could not stop the flow.

If I was not meeting my obligations now, what would happen when the money ran out? What would I do then? In spite of prayer, which I did much of during these times, these thoughts nagged at my mind constantly. The money in and of itself meant very little to me, but the fact that I was not meeting my obligations did bother me. It was my responsibility as a father and husband.

We also had our two dogs with us. Our new-found friends had four or five empty pens in their yard, so we put the dogs in the pens, got unloaded, and tried to prepare for the next step of getting a place of our own.

The following Sunday we went to church, and not long after that we joined. In a way I took a deep breath and sighed, *"Finally, a good, established church. I can settle in and get back on my feet spiritually as well as physically."*

Nathan and Rebekah began to make some friends which was good.

The church was large and a well-established, strong work, but we were not in any shape to serve at this time. I told Terri that, *"If anyone asks you to help in Sunday School or the nursery or wherever, you are to tell them, No."* I knew the condition of my wife, and I knew that she would not be able to say 'no' on her own, so I did it for her.

I did not care what people thought; I knew what was right for us at that time. It was not long after that that she was asked to work in the Sunday School, and she told them, *"No."* They asked why, and she told them that her husband told her not to work in anything at this time.

They did not like that, but I am glad I did it, and she was too.

I began looking for work, but nothing was opening up. I typed up a resume' and put them out all over the place, but no jobs were opening up. When they saw on the application that I had moved up there from California, they would ignore my application. There was a very great resentment to Californians at that time in Washington because so many were moving up there. I have never had a hard time finding a job, but I sure was having a hard time then. The money in our savings kept shrinking little by little.

One day coming home after looking for work I found out that our dog had bitten the garbage man. (I jokingly thought to myself, *"I knew I should have left her on the waterfalls."*) Well, I had to get rid of her. To me a dog that bites is not good to keep, so I took her to this place called "P.A.W.S."

P.A.W.S. reminded me of a liberal, 'feel good about yourself' place. The kind of place that would attract a lot of emotional women. Well, anyway, I brought my dog in, and they were petting her and saying, *"What a nice dog!"*

When they asked me why I was bringing her in, I told them that she had bitten the garbage man.

I have never seen people change so fast from loving to fear.

"Oh no! We have a biter! Keep everyone away from her."

The lady at the front called to the back, *"We have a biter out here."* And a man came out immediately. Of course. I had her on a leash, she wasn't going anywhere, and she was very calm.

After explaining to them that I wanted her put to sleep, they quickly agreed and asked if I would accompany her to the back while they put her to sleep, which I did.

Now, it was just a dog. But it was our dog. It was Nathan and Rebekah's friend through all of the hard times that we had just gone through. Times where tears fell to the floor more often than laughter lifted the roof. It was another event that hurt the hearts of my two children in the middle of having no home, living in a strange house, in a strange place, and now a companion, a friend, had to be put to sleep.

My emotions and my thoughts cried out, *"Lord, what am I doing wrong?"*

In my spare time I split wood for our hosts, and tried to be a help to them as best I could. Much of this time is a fog to me.

My spiritual and emotional state was not good. We all were weary, worn, discouraged and in a state of shock. Why? Because I wanted to serve the Lord Jesus Christ. I wanted to be in His perfect will for my life. I was called to preach and that call burned relentlessly in my bosom and would not let me go. I wanted to get rid of the call at times. I would yell at the Lord, cry, scream, and still the fire burned, *"I must preach."*

I saw the tears of my wife and children, and it broke my heart. I had no answers, and they were looking to me for leadership. I felt sorry for them that they had me as their leader, for I had made their lives a mess.

I had been out of Bible School for nine years. Every decision I had made was an attempt to obey the Lord and do His will. Here I was, no ministry, and up to this point every ministry I had attempted had become an utter failure. I had no job, and couldn't find one. Our money was falling each week, and my family was looking to me for stability, yet I was providing none. My valley continued to deepen, and I began to wonder if I would ever get out of it. It seemed like I was in a pit that continued to grow darker each month.

It was Fall, and we had been living with the Leons now for about a month or two. Nate and Bek each shared a bedroom with their boys and one girl, and

Terri and I slept out in the family room.

We had not rented a place to live yet, for we knew that we needed to wait until I had a job. But no jobs were opening up.

Terri was rapidly reaching the end of her emotional rope. One day Terri told me that she had seen a little house for rent. With excitement in her voice she asked me if I would go and look at it with her, which I did.

It was a clean place with new paint, and in a good location. A small grey house with white trim nestled on a level lot with a few evergreen trees, green grass, and a fenced in back yard. It was the perfect place to live and raise kids.

She longed to have a home again. To cook in her own kitchen, and wash her own dishes. She longed to nest and make a house a home. To tuck her children into their own beds at night.

The rent was high at $750.00 a month. What kind of job would I have to get in order to meet those bills? I had no answer, but I was rapidly losing my authority with my family. I didn't know how we would make it, but I agreed to rent the place.

To get into it took $2,200.00, which I took out of savings, and we moved in. Every day it rained, and then it became cold. The only heating in the house was electric, so our heating bills were in the hundreds, and that was with keeping the temperature at 65 degrees in the day. The money was dropping fast.

During this time I kept looking for work, but I also kept thinking about the Lord's will for my life.

Ah yes! The Lord's will. That aspiration that had brought me into great trouble. That privilege and duty of man. The Lord's will; the reason to be alive.

I kept thinking about evangelism. Over and over in

my mind would be the thought, *"I think that the Lord wants me to be an evangelist, but I'm not sure."* After days of prayer, I decided to call the evangelist that I had in last when my church folded in Twain Harte. I needed someone to talk to about it, and he was the only one I could think of to call.

I gave him a call, and the conversation started with the usual small talk. Then I told him what was in my heart, that I believed the Lord had called me into evangelism. What I wanted him to say was, "I think you are right, and here is what you need to do." But that is not what he said.

I could tell he was sincere, and that he was being as gentle to me as he could, for he knew the trouble that I was going through. But he told me that I was just discouraged, and that the Lord had probably not called me into evangelism.

My heart sank again, and I believed him. I listened to what he had to say and ceased to think of evangelism again. After all, I had been a complete failure in everything that I had tried to do for the Lord. Here was a man that was successful and full time in the ministry. Who was I to be right and him be wrong?

My landlord hired me as a carpenter's helper. I worked for him for a couple of months. It wasn't enough to pay all of the bills, but it slowed the out go of the money. His work ran out, or maybe it was because I almost crushed his leg under a large rock one day. Well, either way, I ended up working for a friend of his who had a landscaping company.

The Pacific Northwest is not a good place to be a laborer for a landscaping company. You see, it rains a lot up there, and whether it is raining or sunny, you have to work regardless.

After nine years out of Bible school, with a Bachelors of Divinity degree, I was weeding flower beds for $6.00 an hour. Because of all of the rain, the flower beds become covered over with moss, and the moss kills the flowers, so the moss must be removed. That can only be done by hand with a Hula hoe.

I vividly remember one day I was doing landscaping work. It was a dull, dreary, rainy day, and I was out in the middle of that dull, dreary, rainy day. I was cold, and soaked to the skin from head to foot, literally. I was cleaning moss out of a flower bed.

Now moss is not very tall, and is not much different than dirt. As a matter of fact, when you Hula hoe it loose from the ground, the bottom half of it is dirt, except in the rain when it becomes mud.

I raked the loose moss into a pile, as the rain dripped off my nose and ran into my eyes. Then I picked the heavy, sloppy muddy moss up and put it in a garbage can that I had by my side for that purpose. I then carried it over to the large trash dumpster in the parking lot. I was soaking wet, the pay was lousy, my heart was in preaching, my finances were a mess, and this valley I was in was getting deeper by the day. *"Lord, what am I doing here? How much lower will this valley go?"* (Oh, I also ended up getting an ear infection after this wet, mud-moss working day.)

With no answers to any of these questions, with my wife wondering what she married, and with the future looking bleaker by the week, I set up an appointment with the pastor of the church we were in.

Terri by this time was losing her confidence in me. Yes, her confidence should be in the Lord, but a wife needs to be able to count on her husband for some things. Everything that I had attempted to do up to that point, except graduating from Bible school, had been a complete failure. It had been nine years of failure after failure, and it was a wonder she did as well as she did. But now her faith in me was slipping, and I could easily understand why.

The evening came for the appointment with the pastor. By this time I was thinking that we needed to get out of the Pacific Northwest. I did not think that we were in God's will, and I did not see how we could make it there because the cost of living was so high.

That evening as I sat in Dr. Ken Blue's office, I stared blankly into space. I had no answers, I was at a dead end. I had given it my all, and failed. Staring down at the floor I said to him, "I know I am saved. I know I am called to preach. Beyond that I do not know anything."

His advice was to settle down, and not to jump around so much, and I can see why he would say that, and somehow I knew that would be what he would counsel. I wanted out of the area.

Terri then listened to his advice and started to encourage me in that direction. How could I say no to her? I had no other answer. But his advice burdened me down so much more. It just didn't seem right, but there was nothing I could do. With so many failures behind me, by this time no one would listen to me, and I had no confidence in my own impressions either.

I agreed, and we decided to buy something in our means, that we could afford. We ended up purchasing a run down mobile home. The plan was to fix it up, sink our roots, and stay for the long haul. The mobile home took just about all of our money in savings. The figurative plane was about ready to touch down.

I had a new job, which was doing what I had done

in California, except the pay was still $6.00 an hour. At night we would work on the run down mobile home, and in the day I would go to work in downtown Seattle.

Still, little things would happen to let me know that something just wasn't right. At one of the hospitals I worked at, I just didn't fit in. Things did not mesh right, though I was trying as best I could.

To get home from work I would ride the bus out to Lynnwood, where my truck was parked. I remember getting on the bus one evening to go home. I grew up in the country so this was all new to me. But I got on the bus and had to stand in the aisle and hold onto the bar. There were people standing behind me, and there were people standing in front of me, and, of course, all of the seats were occupied too.

While standing there feeling like a sardine in a can, the man in front of me begins to fall asleep. His legs start giving out, and he begins to fall back onto me. I felt like I was at the bottom of a tackle football pile and couldn't get my breath. I prayed quietly, *"God, what am I doing here?"* No, this isn't picking up moss in the rain, but it isn't much better. This is crazy!

I recollect another day when it was very cold and cloudy. We were all gathered in the office at 8:00 A.M. for that day's assignments. As our manager was issuing our jobs for that day, I asked, *"What do we do if it snows?"*

So you'll understand, we drove small Mazda pickup trucks with camper shells on the back that carried copy machines in them to take to the hospitals and copy medical records. Seattle is much like San Fransisco. It is a city built on hills. Many of the streets go up and down those mountains, not a good thing to travel on if you have a light-weight pickup truck with no chains on it.

"What do we do if it snows?" My manager looked at me and emphatically replied, *"It NEVER snows in Seattle."* I laughed to myself, for I knew snowstorm weather when I saw it, and this had all of the markings of a snowstorm.

It did snow that day. It started at about 3:00 P.M. and snowed heavily. I quickly finished up work and headed for the office. I clocked out at 4:00 P.M. and walked swiftly to the corner where I would catch the bus. By 4:15 the bus still hadn't come, although they usually came every five minutes. At 4:30 P.M. the bus didn't show, so I started to walk up the bus line to where the bus started its run. By now there were four inches of snow on the roads.

I finally reached the start of the line and with cold and wet feet, I boarded the bus, sat down in the heat and waited to go home. The bus was already almost full, and was full by the time we left. By full I mean that all of the seats were taken, the aisles were full, and even on the entry stairs people were standing. There was no more room for anyone on that bus. Oh, how I hated those buses, especially when they were full!

Little by little we inched our way up 4th Street, the regular bus route. At the next stop we made, the doors opened, but there was no room for anyone to get on, yet one or two literally pushed their way on. A few choice words were spoken, and we inched our way up the road. Cars, trucks, and buses were getting stuck everywhere. I watched a car slide down a hill and crash into another car.

We finally arrived at the next bus stop. The snow

continued to fall heavily. It was what they call an 'Alaskan blast.' By now there were about eight inches of snow on the roads. People lined the sidewalk waiting to get on the bus.

This was downtown Seattle. These were professional people. Ladies in dresses and high healed shoes were standing in the snow as well as men in suits and dress shoes were waiting to get on the bus, but with the bus full, at each bus stop the driver did not open the doors.

The people had been waiting for a long time only to not be able to get on the bus that would take them home. They started to bang on the doors and windows. People from inside the bus started yelling and cussing at them. It was turning into a riot.

Each consecutive bus stop was like that until the driver would allow space in front of him so he could drive past the bus stops. Even then, because our speed was so slow, people would still jump out and bang on the bus as they shouted, *"Stop ______ ______, STOP!!!!"* The windows of the door cracked as fists beat on them.

The bus inched along, and I prayed quietly, *"God, what am I doing here? This is crazy! You called me to preach. What am I doing here?"*

When the bus finally got on the freeway that led up to Lynnwood and the commuter parking lot where our cars were parked, everybody on the bus cheered.

Finally, making it to the parking lot, I got off and the bus left. The other people quickly got in their cars and headed out also. It was cold, windy, and snowy. I had no gloves, nor did I have any really warm clothes on. I got to the truck and with hands already shaking and feeling the bone aching cold, I put the key into the lock to open the door, but it was frozen. It would not open, plus the driver's side lock needed some repair anyway and did not work all that well.

I had one chance left or I would end up very frozen and hurting cold. I had about three ounces of tea left in the jar in my lunch box. I went around to the passenger side of the truck and carefully poured the tea between the glass window and the door of the truck, right over the lock. I stuck my key into the lock, turned it, and praise God the lock opened. *"Thank you Lord!!!"*

I got in, started the truck, and it wasn't long before I was warming up. As the shivering slowly stopped, I thought, *"Whew, that was a close one!"*

Things like that were happening over and over. I started to think back over the year. *"Lord, what am I doing here?"* I came to let the dust settle so to speak and the dust never settled, but more was stirred up.

The intention for which we moved up there had never been fulfilled; God had not allowed it to be fulfilled.

I started to examine things again. *"Am I in God's will or not?"* I came to this conclusion: *"Ken,"* I said to myself, *"I don't think you ever should have left Twain Harte."*

How could I tell Terri that I thought we were out of God's will? We still had not moved into the mobile home that we had just bought, and in her mind we were there to stay. I could easily understand why she felt that way. She had a right to feel that way. I knew I did not have the authority to tell her otherwise. With nine years of failures behind us, and Terri faithfully supporting me all the way, I knew she was at her limit.

From that point on, almost every waking minute I

was in prayer, *"God, we are not in Your will, but I can't tell Terri. Would you please show her that we are not in Your will?"* I prayed and prayed, *"Lord, please help me!"*

After two full weeks of praying, one day, and I think it was at the mobile home as we were working on it, she said to me, *"Ken, I've been thinking, and I don't think we are in God's will. I don't think we ever should have left Twain Harte."*

Oh, that was music to my ears. I told her that it had been two weeks since I thought the same thing, and that I had been praying for her to see it also. She did see it also, and we were back in sinc. My wife and I were back in agreement, praise the Lord.

I called my old boss in Modesto and asked him if he had any job openings. He told me that he did not, and what's more he did not want to hire men for the job because women would not question him as much; the door was closed.

We were now out of money, the savings was empty. I called my Grandma, (Don't use lost relatives!) and asked her if it would be alright if we came back and stayed in her house in Twain Harte until we could get on our feet. She said that would be fine.

Another two weeks went by when my old boss called from Modesto and, with a slight urgency in his voice, asked how soon I could get back there and go to work? The door was open, praise the Lord!

We worked and worked on the mobile home to get it ready to sell. I was so tired of it all. One night at 2:00A.M., I drilled a drill bit into my finger. That was it. *"I quit! Lets get out of here, we've done our best."* With that we left and put the mobile home on the market.

Not many days after, we loaded all of our things into a truck and headed for California, with some assurance that it was the Lord's will. At least it looked like it, and I would be able to support my family. It seemed like a ray of sunlight had broken through the darkness of the storm that had been our life for the last two years.

When we crossed the California line, I stopped at the first rest stop and got out, *"Hello, California! Smell that air,"* I said joyfully and loudly, *"That's the air of California."* Terri was saying, *"Com'on, let's keep going so we can get there."*

Little did I know what would await us in California.

Chapter 10

THE BOTTOM

It was the middle of winter when we arrived back in Twain Harte. A fitting time of year for the trials that we had gone through. Fortunately for us there was no snow on the ground, and we were able to unload our things into a storage unit.

This was the forth move in about a year. The $38,000.00 was now all gone. The mobile home in Washington was on the market, but we had no offers as yet on it. Until it sold we would have a mortgage payment to make. So we had a $500.00 bill to pay, but nowhere of our own to live.

Settling into those familiar surroundings seemed to comfort us a little, but the air was cold, and the house had no insulation. Our breath could be seen rising from our bed in the morning, and there was ice in the sink in the morning.

It was Saturday and only two days since we had been back. I was at work, and everything was going well there.

Rebekah was out riding her little bicycle when a dog ran out in front of her and knocked her off the bike. When she fell, her leg lodged between the front wheel and the frame. As she fell, she fractured her leg.

We took Rebekah to the hospital. After Xrays, they determined it was broken and put a cast on her entire leg. That night she would start to fall asleep and as her body relaxed, she would twitch and then scream out in pain. Terri held her all that night.

The trials would not cease. Just when you would think things could not get any worse, then something else would happen. How far could we go? How bad would it get before we broke?

Two days, later I came home from work to find Terri, Nathan, and Rebekah huddled together on the couch, arms around each other, and it was obvious that they had been crying for a long time.

During the day, my mother and her husband had come up from their house in Scotts Valley, California, three hours away, to stay at Grandma T's house. By now my mother was basically considering it her house since Grandma T was getting up in years.

When they saw Terri and the kids they were furious. Terri and the kids were instantly glad and happy to see them, until they realized the anger was towards them.

Cussing, swearing, and pushing the kids out of the way, they stormed through the house. We were unwanted there, and now we knew it.

After all that we had been through, we come home and even my family did not want us around. We had nothing, and we were unwanted by family. They did not care what we had been through. How could they? They were lost; I couldn't expect them to understand.

What's more is that the Lord was now making it very plain that He did not want us there.

He had been gentle, but because I am dense in the head, He was now going to make it plain.

When Joseph was sold into Egypt by his brothers, he did not end up bitter. When the Lord works it out for him to see his brothers a few years later, he tells them, *Now therefore be not grieved, nor angry with yourselves, that ye sold me hither: for God did send me before you to preserve life.*

For many years I was very bitter towards my family, but I can now see that it was the Lord trying to show me His will for my life, but I did not see it at the time, and neither did Terri, Nate, and Bek.

After yelling and being very ugly to my family, Mom and her husband left. A few days later, my brother and sister came over to the house to talk to me. Terri and the kids were gone by design.

We talked, and they wanted to know when we would be out of the house. I told them that I had asked Grandma T for her permission to be there, but that as soon as I could, I would be out. That is all they wanted to hear.

I remember that meeting. We were homeless basically, yet that did not matter to them, they wanted us out. My own family wanted me out. A very deep wound was struck in me that day.

I know it was a wound that the Lord did not want to put me through, but there was no other way for me to learn the lesson. You see, the Lord was giving me light, even though it hurt more than I had ever been hurt before, yet it was light. At the time I did not see it as light, though that is exactly what it was. If I did not get bitter and quit, I would be able to make it through by the grace of God, and He was going to get me where He wanted me to be.

I had tried working in churches. I had tried working on my own. I had gone back to where I had started. I had taken a church, and every one of these labors ended in complete failure. Now my own family didn't want me or my wife and children around. They didn't care what we had been through. What bothered them is that we were in the way of what they wanted to do.

It was here that my wife began to break. She had all that she could take. With my family doing that to her and the kids, she then looked to her family, her mother.

The next few months were so hard. I don't know what kept us going. There was no Bible believing church to go to, so we didn't go to church. We read our Bibles daily, prayed, and I know that without that we never would have made it through this valley that seemed to go ever deeper.

One evening I told Terri that I wanted to go down to the storage unit. She asked, *"Why?"* I told her that I would like to look at our things.

We all got in the car and went to the storage unit. We opened it, and there in front of us were our things. These were our things, and there were memories attached to them. Memories of love, joy, comfort and a home... our home.

We looked at all the stuff, touched it, and dreamed of having a home someday again. When that would be was unknown. It for sure would not be anytime soon.

These were hard times, and it is difficult to describe what we were up against. We had no money, and what money I did make went to pay the mortgage on a house we could not use. We had no home, and the house we were in, was a place where we were unwanted. Terri would live in fear that family would come by each day. She could not rest there. We had to get out as soon as possible.

My father who lived two miles away would not let us stay there, even though he had plenty of room in his house and had let my brother stay there at times. We were cold, discouraged, and depressed.

With literally all my money going to pay the mortgage payment, I had to get side jobs to make money for food. I had a friend who was a German Baptist, and he did side carpentry jobs. I asked him if he could use a helper, and he said that he could.

My pay was ten dollars an hour, and we were putting a foundation under an old mountain cabin. Many of the old cabins were built on stumps of trees and such. Now, decades later, they were in need of a proper foundation.

More than once I would come home from work, eat, change clothes, take a short nap, go to work under the house for three hours [from 7:00 P.M. until 10:00 P.M.], and then go get paid so we could buy some food to eat.

One evening, already tired from work, plus the stress from the other burdens, and with no money for food, I went over to the house to work. My job was to crawl under the house, which had an eighteen inch crawl space, and with a wonder bar and a hammer I was to dig footers in the dirt for concrete to be poured into.

I crawled under the house and proceeded to work. Outside in the darkness, about 8:30 P.M., it started to rain. A drop light lighted my work area, and with hammer and wonder bar, I dug the hard red clay out to make footers.

I began to cry. *"God, why?"* I asked. *"Every decision I've made I have tried to do what I thought You wanted me to do. I know I have made many mistakes, but Lord it hurts."* There under that house I cried and cried. I worked and cried, and cried and worked. Digging while my my tears watered the dirt that night.

"God I want to serve you. All I want to do is to serve you. Dear Lord Jesus, please help me. I don't know what else I can do. I'm at the end of my rope."

The mobile home was not selling. Things did not look good. Terri had come to her end and had all she could take of the situation. She decided to take the kids and go to Florida to stay with her mother for awhile, at least until I could get things straightened out. She had lost all confidence in me, and I don't blame her. Everything I had tried since leaving school had been an utter failure. Now we were homeless. It had been eleven years of utter failure. I couldn't blame her for wanting to get out of there. They left for Florida, and I ended up sleeping on the living room floor of a friend's mobile home.

I was homeless, and my family was homeless. I had failed to even provide for my family, though I was working as hard as I could. There was nothing more I could do, or at least that I knew of to do.

There was no talk of divorce, though there was some pressure put on Terri by her mother in that direction. I knew her going there would not be good, but again, I had no authority at this time, practically speaking. Scripturally yes, but come on, I could completely comprehend her standpoint. The strain on our marriage at this time was very great.

I would long to talk to her, and in the evening I

would call her, but she would cut the conversations short. John and his wife, Taryn, would be in the living room. I would keep talking as though she was still on the line because I did not want them to know that things were not going well. Again, it was a very hard and fiery trial which was to try me.

One day on my lunch break, I went out to my work car and prayed. I was homeless. My marriage was at the point of collapse. I was broke. I had tried my best to serve my Lord and Savior Jesus Christ, but all I had done for ten years was fail.

As I walked out to the car, I noticed the other cars in the parking lot, and I thought to myself, *"I bet they have houses to live in, and families to go home to."* Sitting down in the driver's seat of that silver Dodge Omni, I bowed my head. I was completely broken and began to pray:

"Dear Lord Jesus, everything that I have ever tried to do was what I thought you wanted me to do. I know I haven't always done it right, but I have tried to. God, it doesn't seem like you even love me."

There was silence in the car for a while as I struggled with anger and bitterness. I was fighting a fight that I had never fought before. I wanted to lash out at God and condemn Him for the way He had treated me, but I knew this was not right. It was not His fault.

I continued in my prayer:

"But the Bible says that You do." After another short space of silence I said, *"and I'm going to believe what the Bible says."*

With great effort, and I emphasize great effort, I made myself say that. I knew I must believe what the Bible said in order to win, for I was at the point of no return if I did not win.

This battle was not with God, this battle was with myself.

This prayer helped me, but the battle was not over. I was at the bottom and there was still more fighting that would take place.

Though the windows were rolled up, for I did not want anyone to hear me, yet there were breezes blowing in that car as if the windows were down. It was something that specifically caught my attention, even though I was in the middle of the battle.

It seemed like a comfort came over my soul.

It also seemed like Egypt was right on my back, or right behind me, and it was saying to me, *"Come back, come back."* But I kept my head bowed and I continued to pray:

"Lord, if there is nothing that I can do for you, then would you please kill me for there is no other reason for me to live than to serve you, and by your grace Lord," I clenched my teeth, tightened my fist and with determination said, *"I am not going back to Egypt, I am not going back to the world!"*

The breezes continued to blow across my face. I prayed again:

"Dear Lord Jesus, everything I've tried to do for you has been a complete failure."

Again there was long silence as I struggled in my soul.

"But if you want me to fail for the rest of my life, Thy will be done! But by Your grace Lord, I am going to get up and try again! I pray all this through Jesus Christ my Savior. Amen!"

I had surrendered to fail for the rest of my life. I meant it then, and there has been no change since I prayed that prayer.

I got out of that car and went back to work, but I believe that the Lord looked at me during that prayer and decided to count me faithful, though it would be a while before I would end up in the ministry. It was in that car, that day, that I was at the bottom of the valley, and yet at the bottom, by the grace of my Lord Jesus Christ, I obtained a great victory.

At the time, it did not seem like a victory at all. I was just getting some things straightened out with the Lord, but I did sense spiritually that something had happened, though I didn't know what.

I still did not know what the Lord wanted me to do, or what His will for my life was, but that was on the back burner for the time. The immediate problems were would I have a marriage? a family? would they come back to California? or would I have to move to Florida?

I did not want to move to Florida, though Terri was leaning that way. I did not think it was the Lord's will, but in my mind there was nothing to stay in California for. I had no spiritual work of any kind going, so in order to save my marriage, I would move back to Florida.

These were very rough days for me. I have never felt stress like I did during those days. After trying my best to provide for my family, and after trying to put the Lord first, I was on the brink of collapse.

Little did I know that during this time, Terri later told me, she had quit on the Lord. She started thinking about going back to the bank where she worked when she was younger. Staying with her mother did not help either, as her mother was working on her to get her to quit on the Lord also.

As I look back, I have no doubt that it was not the

Lord's will for her to go to Florida and stay with her Mom. (Don't use lost relatives when you are in trouble, that is the worst thing you can do.) But Terri had lost confidence in me and went there to get away. Knowing that she was not welcome with my family, caused her to want to leave also.

During her time in Florida she sent me a post card. It was a picture of a dilapidated, old shack where the old, wood siding had grayed from the sun. There were no windows in it, just crooked square holes where there had been some, and there was no door. The whole thing was leaning over about ready to fall down. Weeds were grown up all around it.

On the post card it read, *"Honey, do you think we could afford this?"* She had sent it trying to be funny, but it pierced my heart when I received it. We couldn't even afford that, though I had tried my best to provide for my family.

The stress was obviously evident on my face. I say this because I remember one day at work when I was at the hospital walking up some stairs. As I got to the top of the stairs a man in a white hospital coat was coming towards me. I did not know him, and he did not know me. About fifteen feet from each other we glanced at one another, and I heard him say, kind of to himself, yet audibly, *"I have never seen a face that sad."* I'm sure he saw the hurt and the stress of those times because of the deep "scars" they left on me.

Then one day I heard about a program for low income families to be able to take out a loan and get into a house. I checked on it thinking that because I was not Mexican, or black, that I would not qualify. But as I checked on it, I found out that I did qualify.

I now had something to call and tell Terri. I could

now tell her that there is a good chance that we can get into a house of our own. With that I called her and told her what I had found out, and it did give her some hope.

Looking back I can see that without a doubt the Lord had called me into evangelism by this time, though I still did not see it. But he also remembered that we are dust. Psa. 103:14 *For he knoweth our frame; he remembereth that we are dust.*

We were at our limit of what we could take. I can honestly say that we were sinking emotionally. We were still fighting and giving it all that we could, but our blows, so to speak, had no power left, all strength was gone.

The Lord worked it out for me to fly down to Pensacola and visit. With great resentment, Terri's mother acknowledged me. I spent a week there and then came home. Terri couldn't wait to get back to California too, Praise God!!!

We were still homeless, but we were back together. When they arrived the question arose, where are we going to live? We agreed that Grandma T's was out of the question, so we packed into our friend's mobile home. They will sure get some gold in Heaven! Terri and I slept on the floor of their living room with bugs crawling on us at night.

Then we received word from Washington that our mobile home had sold. When it finally was sold we broke even. There was no equity at all, we were just out from under it. All of our money was officially gone. $38,000.00 was gone in a couple of years, and we had nothing to show for it.

For a long time I was ashamed for having blown it. It bothered me, but then I realized why the money was gone. The Lord had let me use it all up, and He made sure that I used it all up. Why? **Because it was money and profits from lost relatives that's why.** *There was no way He could get any glory from that money, so he would not bless it, and without His blessing it disappeared, just like He wanted it too.*

With my family back in California, we applied for the FMHA loan and we were accepted. Little by little the Lord was helping us climb out of our hole, and it was without the help of lost relatives. He was able to get the glory now so we had His blessing. It makes all of the difference.

Gen. 14:21 And the king of Sodom said unto Abram, Give me the persons, and take the goods to thyself.

Gen. 14:22 And Abram said to the king of Sodom, I have lift up mine hand unto the LORD, the most high God, the possessor of heaven and earth,

Gen. 14:23 That I will not take from a thread even to a shoelatchet, and that I will not take any thing that is thine, lest thou shouldest say, I have made Abram rich.

It had been two months or so that we had been staying with our friends. They were very gracious, but it was not easy on us or them. Since Spring had arrived, Grandma T had now left her winter house, and arrived for the summer back in Twain Harte.

Terri and I talked it over. At first it was out of the question, but with the conditions the way they were, and with the hope of a home loan and a house of our own, we decided to stay with Grandma T until we could get into our own place.

During this time I considered evangelism, and we even looked at a travel trailer. But with no vehicle to pull it, and with the kind of shape we were in, evangelism was not considered long. I do believe that if we would have gone in that direction the Lord would have blessed it, but the call terrified me. I was not sure that I was an evangelist, and even scoffed at the idea as foolish.

I couldn't even pastor a church, and I was going to preach in other churches when I am nothing but a failure? To me it was a crazy idea. We were still homeless, and to family and friends I was a mess, a fool, and a failure.

In September, we applied for a home loan, and it looked likely that we would qualify. The loan program received it's money in the Fall, so that was the time that we had to wait for.

Weeks went by and we heard nothing. During this time we went looking at houses. We got a list of homes that would qualify and proceeded to look at them. Terri went out as I was at work. One day she told me that she had found a home that was not on the list, but would probably qualify for the loan.

To me I did not care about where or what the house was. In my mind we were homeless and needed a house. This was not the time to be picky, but Terri did not look at it that way. She had the emotional side, and had certain things that she wanted.

I was incredulous when I considered the matter. I thought how could she be choosey after all that we had gone through?

We went and looked at the house. It was brand new and had never been lived in. The price was in the range specified on the home loan for us.

Looking through the windows we could imagine where the piano would go. We imagined a fire in the wood stove, cookies baking in the oven, and living in a home of our own.

When we called the owner he said that there were already four others in line for the house. Our hearts sank, and that night we knelt around the bed and prayed with tears, *"Lord I guess it is not Your will for us to get that house. Thy will be done."*

With tears and broken hearts, that night we surrendered not to have a house. We had not heard from FMHA at all, so to us it looked like we were not going to be approved.

Winter set in and it became cold again. Because it had looked like we would be getting a house, we had moved back into Grandma T's while she was up for the summer. Now it was winter, and it was so cold in her poorly insulated home.

During this time we had started attending church again. It was a church that was an hour and a half away. I did what I could in the services which was mainly leading the singing.

It was late Fall, or early Winter, and the house situation did not look good. With the dismal prospect of getting a house, coupled with the fact that we were homeless, or should I say that it would be easy to leave, it seemed like all these things pointed towards the field of evangelism. With that situation before me, I then thought of all the signs and events of the past ten years that seemed to point towards evangelism. Along with this was the nagging feeling that I was an evangelist. (Some people are really slow.)

I talked to the pastor of the church we were attending, and he seemed positive towards the pursuit of evangelism. This was something that had never happened before. I now had a successful man in the ministry who was encouraging me and was willing to help me get into evangelism. Not long after that, on a Sunday morning, I took Terri and the kids forward in the invitation and publicly professed the call to evangelism.

The pastor began to help us as best he could. He let me preach in the church a few times, and it always went well. We had pictures taken and a letter written to send to churches letting them know of my call to evangelism.

At the same time, though, I had mentioned to pastor Nichols, of the need for a good Bible believing church in the Sonora area. There was a man who had planted many churches in the central California area, so I went to him to see if he would be willing to come over and start a church in Sonora. He had experience, and the Lord had greatly used him to start churches.

It was not convenient for me to go see him, and he made no effort to come see me. I went after work and arrived at his house around 8:00 P.M. and left about 10:00 P.M., which put me home after 11:30 P.M. This was all the Lord showing me that He was not in it; I did not see that. All I could think of was that my home area had no Bible believing church and my heart was burdened for it.

The meeting went very poorly, as all he wanted to do was argue with me about Ruckmanism and dispensationalism. I received no help or encouragement from him at all. I left that night, again perplexed, that he had no burden for the Sonora area.

Now, with the intention of evangelism, the need for a church in the Sonora area did not effect me as much. But the burden was there, nonetheless. And it was a heavy burden at times.

The church we were attending was going to have

special services. Some local pastors would be at the meeting and there would be special music as well. It was really a mini revival meeting. I was anticipating meeting some pastors with the thought that maybe the connections would work into some of my own meetings as an evangelist.

We attended the services, excited about the thought of hearing the preaching, and possibly getting a little help in the call to evangelism. After the preaching that evening, a very well-known and succesful preacher in the area came up to me. As he came up to me, he said in a pastoral sort of way, *"Brother Ken, I heard you are considering evangelism. I don't think that is what you ought to do. We need a church over in Sonora. I think the Lord wants you to start a church over there. I do not think you should pursue evangelism. You know, we need more good churches around here."*

Well, I could not argue with that, but my heart sank again. Here was another good man who was in the ministry, and I was not. I did not have the confidence to disagree with him. I listened to what he had to say, and I accepted his advice. I would not pursue evangelism any further. After all, he was successful, and I was a miserable failure, at least that is how I looked at it.

He said that they would get a bus load of people together to come up to Sonora to help us let the people in the area know of our new church. This offer never materialized, for when he looked at a map he decided that it was too far for his people to come, but the damage had already been done. I had ceased , again, to pursue evangelism. Pastor Nichols agreed that we needed more churches, and his encouragement towards evangelism stopped.

Winter set in and we were back at Grandma T's freezing in the uninsulated house. What's more we were out of fire wood.

Nathan and I would go down the backside of the property, which was a very steep hill, and cut wood. Have you ever cut wood on the downhill side and had to haul it up the hill? It is not easy, nor fun. I rigged up Nathan's wagon with a pulley system. With 300 feet of rope, I tied one end of the rope to myself and the other end to the wagon. As I walked backwards down the hill, the wagon would go up the hill with one or two large rounds of wood on it. I literally was a dumb waiter! The rounds were about three feet in diameter. I told Nathan that if the wood got out of control, or if anything went wrong, to just get out of the way. In less than ten feet, a round of wood could pick up such a momentum that it could easily kill a person if it hit them and knocked them down.

With the make shift pulley system, we worked to get the wood up the hill. Then on top we had to split it, and use it in the fireplace. It was very hard work, but at least it was free, which is what I could afford at the time.

These were days of hardship that went on and on. The house was cold, and the wood was a labor that didn't meet the need on the real cold days. My job was steady, but I would still need to work side jobs on Saturday to make ends meet and climb out of the hole we were in.

Hope of ever getting a place of our own was a fanciful dream. The desire to preach was becoming a tormenting burden that would never go away because it came from the inside. There was no where I could go to get away from the push, the desire, the burning in my heart that seemed to drive me to the call of, *"I must preach."*

The ministry was becoming a fading dream. Failure, failure, that is all I knew. God's will for my life was something that I had no idea of how to find, and something that seemed like I never would find. I was eleven years out of Bible school and a miserable failure.

Chapter 11

BACK ON OUR FEET

The future looked so dark. After surrendering to not getting the house we had looked at, now we were at the point of surrendering to not having a house at all. What do I do? Where do I go? Lord what is Your will? Why is all of this happening? So many never ending questions ran through my mind.

Then one day in November 1990, we received a phone call. It was the owner of the house that we had been so excited about. He said that all of the other buyers had backed out and that the house was available if we wanted it.

As I talked to him on the phone my heart sank again. What could I say? Yes, we wanted it, but there was no way for us to get it. I told him that we were not interested because we did not have the financing to get it. We had given up on FMHA, thinking that it was a dead end. The house that we had so hoped for was now available, but we could not get it.

It is hard to put into words the condition we were in, but I must say that it was a condition that if something did not happen in our favor, we would not recover. There would be permanent damage to us that would never be undone in this life.

You may ask, *"What kind of damage?"* I must say that I don't know. Maybe emotional or spiritual, I'm not sure. But since those days Terri and I both have talked about this time, and we both know that it was a time when we were right on the edge of falling over a cliff that would have been a cliff of no return.

I know that with God all things are possible, but I'm telling you it seemed like something would have happened that would have ruined us for full service for the Lord from that day forward, had the Lord not stepped in.

Looking at this time I believe that the reason we were having such a hard time getting into a house was because the Lord wanted us in evangelism, which I did not see. It would have been God's perfect will, I have no doubt, to enter evangelism at this time. I believe it was God's perfect will to enter evangelism when I surrendered to it in Washington the first time.

But I had been talked out of it three times now, so I did not consider evangelism as God's will for my life.

Ah yes! God's will for my life. That pinnacle of service. The utmost privilege for mortal man to do something for his creator. Yes, the will of God.

I was still in pursuit, but my steps were beginning to falter. If you would have been able to see my steps, as a hunter tracks an animal, you would have seen that I was staggering, weaving from weak and weary legs that had little strength left. I, and my family, pressed on, as if on autopilot, but we were on the edge of a great cliff that we would not have come back from if we went over.

Our Lord Jesus Christ knew this, and though I do not believe that it was His perfect will, yet He knew we were at the end of ourselves. He knew that we had given all that we had, and we had given it for Him. It had not been in His perfect will, but He knew our hearts, and He knew we needed to heal.

Less than a week after receiving the phone call from the owner of the house telling us that it was back on the market, we received a letter from FMHA telling us that we were fully approved to buy a house.

I was standing in the dining room with the family all around me as I opened the mail. The letter from FMHA had stimulated all of our curiosities. The kids looked up at me, and Terri looked on as I read the letter. Then with astonishment I said, *"We qualified!? Hallelujah!" We can get the house!* Joy and excitement sprang into all of our faces.

Immediately I called the owner of the house and asked if it was still on the market........ and it was!!!! It looked GOOD! I told him that we were approved and had the financing in place. It looked like we were going to get a home. A home of our own. Without the help of lost relatives.

Now we had hope, and with hope life is a little easier to bear. We could see an end to our bleak condition in sight.

The frozen ice in the sink in the morning and the coldness of the house was a bit more bearable knowing that we would have a house.

Often we would go over and look through the windows like we had done before, but now there was more excitement and joy for it would be ours. That winter, though we were cold, yet it didn't seem as bad, knowing we would have a house to live in. The winter passed and early spring was upon us. Nathan started playing baseball.

I was leading singing at the church in Jackson, over an hour away. Because of the distance we never felt a part of the church, though the people were very friendly to us.

Spiritual things had always been the most important part of our lives. Church, Bible reading, prayer and living for our Lord Jesus Christ always came first. But with the hardship and need for a place of our own, these things were put on a 'back burner' so to speak, but they were not pursued with as much zeal as they had been at other times.

For me, I looked at it as I was not doing my duty as a man to provide for my family. Because of this, the burden to get into a place and provide for my family was just as great as my desire to preach and serve the Lord. The Bible says that no man can serve two masters, for either he will love the one and hate the other, or else he will hold to one, and despise the other. There was a wrestling going on, and at times I resented the call to preach.

I had given it my best for over eleven years, and every try was a failure. A fisherman will come home from fishing and hold up his stringer of fish, or you will see pictures of stringers of fish that were caught. My stringer was a stringer of failures from start to finish. I had nothing to hold up and show.

With this discouragement welling up in me, with the trials that I had put my family through, and with the guilt of not providing for my family, some of the spiritual things were let to slip, but thank God for His care for us.

One day I had heard that the Oakland A's baseball team was having a 'meet the players' day for little league baseball players. Nathan had been playing baseball in little league so he would qualify. There was just one problem, the game was on Sunday.

My deceitful and desperately wicked heart went to work on how I could take Nathan to the game. Reasoning with myself I thought, *"Well, I'm not preaching, I'm only leading the singing, and they have others that can do it. It's not that big of a deal."* (Let me emphasize that this reasoning is not right.) My reasoning continued. *"We have been through a lot of trials, and I have never been to a major league baseball game anyway. Let's get some memories as a family, after all, Nate will be grown before I know it, so I had better get the memories while I can."* Also using scripture to justify my actions, I quoted to myself Rom. 14:5 *"One man esteems one day above another, another man esteems every day alike."* Sunday is no different than Wednesday or Saturday.

There, I did it, and I even had scripture to back it up. Now I can go to the game with a clear conscience, well... kind of.

I bought the tickets for the game, and we got ready to go. We were all excited, especially Nathan. Mark McGuire and Jose' Canseco were on the team, and I think Ricky Henderson was on the team at that time also.

Saturday came and we were getting things packed for the game. We would have to leave fairly early on Sunday to get there at the right time. Oakland, California was about three hours west of us.

About 4:00 P.M. in the afternoon, I just did not feel good. My stomach felt upset. Terri agreed that hers didn't feel good either. An hour or two later Nathan and Rebakah also felt like they did not feel good.

Now, I am not one to puke. As a matter of fact, I hate to puke. I will do everything I can to make it go the other way. But around seven that evening there was no keeping it down. I knew that whatever was in my stomach was coming back up and out through my mouth.

Bent over in the bathroom into the toilet, I emptied the contents of my stomach. It was not too long after that that Terri went into the bathroom and did the same thing. Then it was Nathan followed by Rebekah. Throughout that night we all took turns at the bathroom. Sometimes it was 'hurry up, I can't wait.'

Then it turned to dry heaves; there was nothing left to come out, just the yellowish mucous stomach lining, at least it felt like that. Terri said that she had never before in her life puked as hard as she did that night.

My sides hurt as I lay there in bed that Sunday morning. We were all exhausted. Groans emanated from each of our beds as we lay there with our sides aching from the extreme use of the muscles our bodies involuntarily made us use throughout the night.

We did not go to the baseball game that Sunday. We did not go anywhere that Sunday. But as I lay there thinking, tears welled up into my eyes. I knew that the Lord had chastened us for skipping out on church. It was His love for us that had caused Him to deal with us so, and I knew it. I prayed there as I lay and said, *"Thank you Lord for caring for me and dealing with me. Thank you for showing me that I needed to take my family to church, and that it is not just any other day."*

It was early Spring, and finally our day came in

April. We were able to move into our new home. A home no one else had ever lived in.

We had slept on floors, abandoned office rooms, other people's beds and houses. We had slept with bugs crawling on us. It had been about a year and a half that we had been homeless, and now we were getting into a real house of our own. Three bedrooms and two baths, a wood stove, a kitchen and a small porch to sit out on and hear the wind play a song on the needles of the pine trees. We were home, glory to God!

The house was up on a ridge. A very short walk up the easement and you could see for miles. You could look over the San Joaquin Valley of California. Hawks and eagles would soar on the updraft that ascended from the sides of the valley, and at times, because the ridge was so high, you would be looking down on them as they glided in the currents. The sunsets were beautiful as well.

We had moved into our new found refuge, our new found hospital, for it was a place that we would heal from the wounds and hardship of the past years.

Not long after moving into our new house, we had an old problem come up. Again, our neighbors were rotten. They greatly resented us moving into the house and spoiling their privacy.

Again I had to confront them on various things that they were doing to make our life hard. Property line issues and various other things were always causing a problem.

I can see now that the Lord was not going to let us get too comfortable in our new house.

Other than that, the days we lived in that house in Ponderosa Hills were good days. Days of many good memories; memories that were allowed by the grace of God, even though I was not in His perfect will.

Terri home schooled our kids, and every now and then I would come home to a new story of what had happened that day.

One dog had made it all the way with us and that dog was Chauchie, a brown short terrier mix, with ears like a German Shepherd's. She almost looked like an overgrown rat with big ears. We then got another dog, a golden lab retriever mix. During the day the kids would take a break from school and get the dogs playing and running. Chauchie was the kind of dog that had to have everything in control, so when they got going she would get upset and chase Goldie, the lab, around the house.

Screams of laughter and cheers would be heard from the house as Chauchie chased Goldie around the living room couch. Goldie would lower her rear end as Chauchie would nip at her heals. Around and around they would run with the kids and Terri laughing the whole time. It was a time of healing.

Rebekah was learning to play the piano. We had a cat name Scrawney because he had been the runt of the litter. Scrawney was the best cat I had ever seen, and he had the greatest personality of any cat I had ever known.

When Rebekah would play the piano, Scrawny would put his paws on the arm rest of the couch and his back feet on the cushion sitting up facing the piano and listen to Rebekah play.

The smell of fresh cinnamon rolls made from scratch, or poppy seed bread would often fill the house as Terri baked them in the oven.

On Friday nights I would drive up to Twain Harte

straight from work, to where Rebekah was taking piano lessons. Terri and Nathan would be there also.

After piano lessons and dinner with her piano teacher, (dinner that Terri would have already cooked and brought to the lesson), then it was our special trip home. Because I had my work car, we then had two cars to go home in.

Jumping in the car, Rebekah and I would speed down the hill looking for a place to hide in the darkness of night. Finding just the spot, we would quickly pull into it and turn the lights off and wait. If Terri and Nate found us, they would point their lights on us. Then they would speed off, and we would try to find them.

The kids would scream with excitement as we did this each Friday night on the way back to our home in the hills. It was a time of healing that we so desperately needed.

I planted a garden and also Redwood trees up on a hill. We watched the fog roll up the valleys, but now we looked over the top of it. It looked like a white misty ocean of waves with islands of mountain tops peeking through to the sunshine and blue sky.

It snowed, so Terri and the kids went sledding down the hill right next to the house. They laughed and screamed as the saucers flew down the hill. *"Let's double up"* they said, so Terri and Nate went down together, laughing the whole way.

My family would attack me. One child on each arm, and my wife gave orders to tackle me. *"Let's get him down and tickle him."* It was a dog pile that rolled around the living room floor with dogs barking, and laughter sounding out through the walls of our new found refuge. It was a time to heal.

It had been so hard, yet we were, physically, back on our feet.

Chapter 12

JUBILEE BAPTIST CHURCH

We were now on our feet, but why were we there? I had no idea. What the Lord wanted me to do I was not sure of. But I could now think about it more knowing that I was providing for my family like I should.

About this time the pastor of the church in Jackson started to become much more domineering in his pastoring. I was still leading singing even though the church was about an hour and fifteen minutes away. The pastor began to demand that I go soul winning even though we lived that far. He told me that I could not lead singing if I did not go soul winning.

I asked him if I could go over in the Sonora area, and he said no, that I had to go in his area. To me this was a very unreasonable burden that he was putting on me. Often my job took me over 200 miles a day, and then to add this to my schedule was just too much. I told him that I could go on Sunday afternoons, and he agreed to that.

This got me to thinking though. Pastor Seers had said that we needed a church over in the Sonora area. I am over there, and this time I am not using relatives. I prayed and prayed, *"Lord, do you want me to start a church over there?"*

About this time the family that had left my church right at the end, at the start of the revival, started coming around. After some apologies it seemed like they wanted to start a church. We started having services in our home, and they seemed to go well.

I have no doubt that at this point the Lord just started shaking his head. I wonder if He said to Gabriel, *"He is one of the slowest, most hardheaded, densest sons, that I have ever dealt with!"* Gabriel surely replied, *"One thing is for sure Lord, he sure doesn't catch on too quick!"*

When we started having services, Terri said to me, *"I will wash your clothes, and cook your meals, and do what I am to do around the house. I will get the kids ready and attend the services, but I will not do anything in the church."*

It didn't surprise me because of what we had already been through. It was my call anyway, not hers.

One Sunday morning we were having services in our living room. It was a very nice day, so I left the front door open. As our neighbors heard the singing they got very upset and complained to the County about us having church in our home. The County called and told us that we were not zoned for a church and had to stop.

After prayer, we decided to move the church to a shopping center, and I named it Jubilee Baptist Church. Was it the Lord's will to start a church? Looking back I must say it probably was not. But thank God for Romans 8:28 *And we know that all things work together for good to them that love God, to them who are the called according to his purpose,* because there were a few blessings from the time that I tried to pastor that little church.

We started holding services in the store front, and things seemed to go well. Some of my old members from Twain Harte were attending, along with some new people.

Nathan had been on a baseball team. His coach was a man by the name of Russ Ford. From all appearances Russ did not appear to be saved. His wife, Joan, would help out with the baseball practices also.

One day in a baseball game, Nathan was the pitcher. Before each pitch he would turn around and bend over. His coach, Russ, wondered if he was hurt, or what he was doing?

Russ called time out to the referee and walked out to have a talk with Nathan. He came up to Nate and asked if he was alright. Nate replied that he was. Russ then asked, *"Well, I see you bending over before each pitch, what are you doing?"* Without a hesitation Nathan replied, *"I'm praying for a strike."*

With great surprise and amazement Russ returned to the dugout. He related the incident to me, and from that incident Russ and Joan started coming to church. It turned out that Russ was saved, but severely backslidden, though his wife Joan was not saved.

In time Joan called me, and we set up a time to meet at the church. She had questions about salvation. There in that little store front Joan asked Jesus Christ to be her Savior.

When she had finished praying, we talked a little,

and then she went home. But there was no emotion, or any outward sign that Joan got saved. It was over the next few weeks that I could see that she was not the same. She really had meant it, and she was obviously saved.

The church was doing well. The little storefront was filling up, and it was exciting to see. Jubilee Baptist Church was now about a year and a half old. With the new people that had been saved was the need for them to get baptized. Without a baptistry in the church, I decided to have one outdoors in public, which is the reason for baptism anyway-- a public profession and identification with Jesus Christ.

I gave the announcement and the date was set along with the place. We would have a baptism at Pinecrest Lake, which was a public lake located at about a 5,000 foot elevation, and a very beautiful place. It was also a very busy place in July, and that is when we had the baptismal service.

There was one lady who had started coming, and she had been a Mormon. I announced that no bathing suits were to be worn at the service, or by any of us that day up there. We were to be a testimony. But I could tell she was going to wear one anyway. Preachers can tell things, and I knew she intended to go against what I had announced.

The Sunday before the baptismal service, I preached on Biblical nakedness and aimed at her with the word of God and fired. Oh, I hit a bull's-eye, and she and her husband never came back to church. That was not my intention, but that was the result.

The baptismal service went well with a hundred or so lost people lining up on the beach to watch. Some asked what we were doing as they had no idea what baptism was all about. We witnessed to them, but no one got saved.

There had been two single people coming to church at this time. They would travel from Jackson and had been attending the church there, but because of the domineering attitude of the pastor, they decided to come over to Jubilee.

After the July baptismal service, they had both already decided and planned to leave for Bible school. I knew about it, so this service was also a sort of going away fellowship for them also.

Praise the Lord they both are serving the Lord today. One is a full time missionary, and the other is working in the prisons.

At the time, they were both single, and very dedicated to the Lord, and to the work of the Lord Jesus Christ. They both were going to be missed, but I had no idea just how much we all would miss them.

Chapter 13

GOD'S WILL, FINALLY!

The little storefront church we called Jubilee Baptist Church started to slide. Russ and Joan bought a restaurant and could not make it to the services. Another man died and his wife flipped out. Another man was a Calvinist, and we conflicted: he and his wife left. Little by little attendance was dropping. The joyful fellowship of the saints was turning quickly into the endurance of the saints.

One Sunday morning this widow, whose husband's funeral I had preached two weeks earlier, comes into my little storefront church of about twenty people. She had stick-on name tags in her hand, and with a take charge attitude, proceeded to start writing our names on the tags and sticking them on each of us. It was still early with about thirty minutes before the services began.

I couldn't believe what she was doing. We didn't need name tags for twenty people. What was I to do? I prayed and went up to her and told her that we did not need name tags, and that I did not want her doing that. Oh My! She went to pieces and started crying, *"I was just trying to help,"* she replied with a quivering voice and tears beginning to run down her cheeks. I told her that I knew she meant well, but I didn't think we needed those name tags.

The one other family that was there went to pick up someone, so I was in our little church, Sunday morning, with some young kids and this lady who was crying. Well, what should I do? I didn't know what to do, but to let her cry. I guess she needed a hug, but I wasn't going to do that.

I picked up my guitar and started to play some songs thinking that it might get a better spirit in the building. But I had forgotten one verse, Prov. 25:20 *As he that taketh away a garment in cold weather, and as vinegar upon nitre, so is he that singeth songs to an heavy heart.*

She turned her face to the window and sobbed as I sung about the Lord. A few minutes later she walked out of the church and never came back. At least now I didn't have to worry about having to walk around the church, as its pastor, with my own name tag on.

Wednesdays I would be the only one there with my family, and Sunday evenings we would be there with only one other family. I ended up canceling Sunday evening services.

For the next year and a half there was no movement, no conviction, no one saved. It was a very spiritually dead church. A few in the church became disgruntled and left. Little by little it was slipping, and I knew the signs by now. I had experience with churches that were going nowhere but down.

I was now thirteen years out of Bible school. The

desire to preach was still there, and the desire to do God's will still filled my thoughts daily. Again, I was frustrated and very discouraged.

I looked around and I could see other churches growing. I could see other independent Bible believing churches that were growing, but mine wasn't growing. The other churches were growing, and they had not compromised at all in order to get it to grow. I saw that and wondered why my church was not growing.

I thought to myself, *"It obviously can be done, for there are other churches that are growing. What is the problem?"* I did something very different than I had ever done before in all of those thirteen years of failure. I began to pray a prayer that went something like this:

"Dear Lord Jesus, something is wrong. I see other churches growing, or at least functioning the way they should, but mine is not. Lord, I know something is wrong, and **I know it is me**. *If others can make it and I can't, then the problem is me. I know it can be done, but not by me. Lord, what's wrong?"*

I prayed that way for some time. I thought and thought about what the problem could be, but I had no idea. Here I was thirteen years out of school and my fourth church was going down. Another failure on top of all the rest that I had ever since graduating from Bible school. Graduation was the last success that I had had. The difference now was that **I knew that I was the problem.**

I did not blame it on the hardness of the last days, or the wickedness of the people around me. I knew it wasn't because of the wickedness of America, or other such excuses. I had absolutely no doubt that I was the problem. Beyond that knowledge I had no answer, but at least I had that much light.

Maybe I would have to fail for the rest of my life. Again, I was low in spirit. My family had never seen me succeed at anything. For thirteen years Terri had been with me, but had never seen me succeed. She was loosing her faith in me, and really figured I would never make it in the ministry. My children had never seen me succeed. I was losing respect in their eyes.

My job was steady, but I had climbed as far as I could go, there were no more raises left. I prayed and seriously considered starting my own business, but every time the Lord obviously said, *"No!"* I had been running my district by myself, and knew exactly what to do. But God would not let me do it.

On every side it seemed like things were not going well. My life was a life of frustration. There was a drive, a desire, a longing and a calling that stirred me from within. Yet, all I was doing on the outside to fulfill God's call, and to pursue that desire, that burning from within, was getting thwarted at every turn.

At times the atmosphere at home was not good. I was short with the family, and they would scatter when I walked through the door from work. Later in the evening, I would apologize for my attitude. I didn't yell, or hit anyone, but I was not a pleasure to have around either.

Day in and day out, the thought of *"I must preach"* was there, but it seemed like God was not.

One evening I received a phone call. It was the pastor over in Jackson. Pastor Nichols had left the church and this was a new pastor. He asked me if I would preach for him on Thursday evening. His church had a Thursday evening service, instead of Wednesday evening. I said that I would be glad to preach for him, and it was set for the next week.

Preaching by now had lost its thrill. It was something that I did because I was supposed to. To try to minister to the people with the word of God was beyond my consideration at this point.

It was like I was in a boxing match and I was swinging, but there was no power in any of my punches. My opponent was playing with me, toying with me like a cat plays with a mouse. Those watching what was going on would laugh like the Philistines as they made sport of Samson. But my opponent was unseen, elusive and wearing me down.

Who was my opponent? Was it God? No, it couldn't be. Was it the Devil? My attitude at the time was, maybe, but I don't think so. Sure the Devil would work on me, as would the world and the flesh. But I sensed that there was something more. There was something wrong, but I really had no answer, and I really was losing all hope.

Though very low in spirit, I remember really wanting to do my best for that Thursday evening service. I prayed, studied, and put together a sermon. Looking back, I don't think it was much of a sermon, but I really had tried to do my best for my Savior. That Thursday we left for Emmanuel Baptist Church in Jackson, California, and though I was discouraged, yet in my heart, I was intent on doing the best I could do.

When we arrived, we saw old friends from when we had been there. It was so good to see them again. The service started with the usual singing, and then it was time for me to preach.

I started my sermon and did my best. It was a sermon like any other. A sermon no different than the hundreds that I had preached for the last few years at Jubilee in Sonora. It was just another sermon, like just another day at work, or just another load of laundry that had to be done. This is how I looked at it.

At the end of the sermon, I gave the usual invitation to come forward and pray at the altar (because that's what you do at the end of a sermon). I was going through the motions like it was an old habit, and you don't even have to think when you do it.

The invitation was for the people to come and make things right with the Lord, if he has dealt with any of the people about anything. Did I expect Him to have dealt with anyone? No! Did I even consider that the Lord would deal with anyone from my sermon? No!

To me it was the end of another sermon, which was the end of another service, and then we would go home.

But that night something happened that at first startled me, and then surprised me. People started coming forward to the altar. I hadn't seen that happen for well over a year. I slightly jumped, due to surprise, when some people walked down the aisle, though I don't think anyone saw me.

I can't believe it! Someone was touched by the sermon? People's hearts had been touched and now they were coming and kneeling at the altar to get things right! Out of the thirty people that were there that night, about six or seven were kneeling at the altar. My spirit quickened, and my heart beat faster, as joy filled my soul to think that someone had been helped by a sermon that I had preached, that maybe the Lord had used me that night in the lives of a few people.

That's all I wanted, to be used by the Lord. What a privilege; what a joy! And that night He had used me a little, for His glory.

Then I remembered as they were coming forward, *"Oh yeah, that's what is supposed to happen."*

The service ended, and we started on our hour and a half trip to our home.

My mind started racing. People were actually touched tonight! I thought of Lisa saying, *"I always thought he was an evangelist."* Then I thought of Grandma saying in her high, sweet, squeaky voice, *"I always thought that's what you should do."* I thought of being introduced as Evangelist Ken McDonald at Bro. Smith's. I thought of the meetings in other pulpits that had always gone well; how Valley Springs went well until I took it as pastor.

I thought of when I surrendered to evangelism and so on. I thought of how every church I had taken was a failure. Light began to dawn on me with the thought that, *"Maybe I am an evangelist?"*

I started thinking out loud, talking to Terri as I drove. My words were flowing out as fast as my thoughts. Then I got silent for a bit. A realization came over me, and an understanding quickened me that I saw as straight from my Lord Jesus Christ.

I remember the spot, it was just a few miles west of Jackson that with astonishment I said, *"You know, I think I am an evangelist."* Then with a firm resolve, I said, ***"AND I DON'T CARE WHAT ANYBODY SAYS!"***

I can't say that I heard the voice, but as clear as ever, it seemed like I sensed the Lord say, *"Well, it's about time!"* And a peace flooded my soul from the realization that it was the Lord's will for me to be an evangelist.

This time it was different. My sight, my heart, my intention were all in relation to my Lord and Savior

Jesus Christ this time. From here on I would pursue this call as coming from the Lord. As such, I did not need any encouragement from any man, for I was walking on the light I had received from the Lord directly, and that made all the difference to me.

It had been thirteen long, arduous years of pain, toil and failure. I often think about those years, and the fact that if I had quit, I never would have found God's will for my life. If I would have quit, not being willing to sell all I had, nor to sacrifice all I could in order to press on for the light I needed to KNOW God's will for my life, then I never would have found it.

Ah yes! God's will! That lofty duty of man to perform. That specific job the King of the universe, Jesus Christ wants you to do for Him. The King and Savior who bought you, if you are born again, with His blood that He shed on Calvary to pay for your sins. Ah yes! God's will! The reason, and purpose I am alive, I finally found His perfect will for my life.

Chapter 14

GOD'S HELP

I cannot say that I did not have my doubts, for I did. After so many years of failure you begin to second guess yourself on everything. I knew, though that my church was going to fail, and that I had to at least attempt to pursue evangelism.

Not long after surrendering to my new-found call as an evangelist, I received a phone call from a church in Modesto to come and preach for a service. This was completely unsolicited, and seemed to greatly confirm that I was at least headed in the right direction. The meeting went well.

It was time to close Jubilee Baptist Church. There was one family that had stayed with us, and I knew it would be hard for them. I did not look forward to telling them that it was over.

On a Wednesday evening, Mike came to church and it was just him and I there. We were sitting down on the front pew, and I told him that the church would be closing. He looked a little down. I then told him that

I believe God wanted me to be an evangelist. When I said that his head jerked slightly, and an astonished realization came over his face as he said to me, "*You know what? You're right! That is what you should be.*"

It was another confirmation that I was headed in the right direction. Wonder, excitement and fear all filled me during this time.

The evangelistic call still terrified me as much as ever. I was still extremely intimidated by it. But the light I had gave me enough faith that it was the Lord's will for my life to press on in that direction.

What do you do? How do you attempt to enter the ministry of evangelism without a home church, and also starting from California. I knew the average pastor back east thought of California as 'can any good thing come out of California?'

I sent out a prayer letter introducing myself as an evangelist. With 135 churches' addresses which I had collected from the missionaries that we supported, I mailed them out. Out of the 135, two of them were in the east, the rest were west of the Mississippi.

Standing at the mailbox, holding the letters in my hand I looked at them. I dropped the 133 letters in the box with no problem. I then held the two that were addressed to the east. One was to upstate New York, and the other was to Southern Florida. As I looked at them I honestly thought to myself, "Well, no one is going to contact me anyway, don't worry about it."

Out of those 135 letters, I got three back, one of which was from Texas, and the other two were from Upstate New York, and Southern Florida. When I received them it really shook me up. What would I do?

I had two weeks of paid vacation coming, so I decided that I would use them for my first trip in evangelism, and that trip would be to Texas. I scheduled the meeting with the church, and then another church in the area asked if I would come and preach for them? I had just enough time, and it would help pay for the expense of the trip by providing two offerings instead of one.

I had a problem, though. At the time, our car was a Geo, three cylinder tin can, that the four of us could barely fit into. I prayed, *"Lord, how are we going to make it to Texas in that?"* Nathan's knees were almost in his chin when he road in the back seat.

This greatly troubled me, and then one day on the way to work, I saw the answer to my problems. There on the side of the road, in the Safeway parking lot, was an Oldsmobile Cutlass for sale. I pulled in and looked at it, and it looked real good for the price, but I decided that I would not make a rash decision. I would go to work, and if it was still there when I came by on my way home, then I would check into it.

I prayed and prayed that day, and on the way home I saw that it was still there. After calling and meeting with the owner, I took it for a test ride. It seemed real nice. I prayed and decided that I would make an executive decision without any consultation, *"I'll take it."* I put it on my credit card; not a good idea!

Well, I drove it home, which was an hour away. I flipped the electric locks up and down. I rolled the electric windows up and down, *"hum, niiiccceee!!!!"* With eager anticipation I imagined the look on Terri's and the kids' faces as I pulled into the driveway. Boy, was I going to surprise them!

Finally, coming home I pulled right up in front of

the window where I knew that Terri would be, and would be able to look out. She looked up, and when she realized it was me, she immediately came out. Looking the car over she asked, *"Are you taking it for a test drive."*

I had turned the car off, but as she asked me the question there was a bit of gurgling starting to emanate from within the bowels of the engine. In response to her, I replied just as proud as a peacock, *"No Honey, I bought it."* As I said that there was a rather loud sploosh, and hot water came pouring out from under the hood. I couldn't believe it. After a rather large repair bill, we had a good car.

Loaded up, we headed for Texas with my new realization that I was an evangelist. Upon arrival we met the family, and they were real good folks. I had gone to school with him. His was the car that ran on five cylinders. They had a large family so funds were low. They gave us their best and we had good fellowship with them.

It was hot when we were there, and they did not have air conditioning, so the front door was open with a screen door on it. They told us of how a few nights earlier a snake had crawled into the house. Wasps hovered around the lights and windows, and each night we slept on the floor. The cushions were pulled off the couch, and I slept on them, but you know? I slept better those nights than I had in a long time for I was right in the will of God.

The meeting went very well, and they asked us to come back again.

We went onto the next meeting, which was not that far away. They also gave us of their best, and the meeting went very well. At this meeting, though, we slept in the living room, and the preacher's wife would come out early in the morning and start cleaning the kitchen; and one morning she even started cleaning out her refrigerator which was two feet from my head. I told Terri, *"Let's get out of here,"* and we would be gone for the day.

Eventually, more meetings came in. With the meetings scheduled, it was now time to take our first trip around the United States of America.

I took Terri out on the ridge, and we talked about it. I told her that we had a choice; she and the kids could stay home until the ministry built up, or we all could go together. I then told her that we got married to be together, so *"You and the kids are going with me. We may sleep on floors or in campgrounds, but having food and raiment let us be therewith content.*

Before we left, it looked like we would not be able to make the house payments. I told Terri that we might lose it all again, but I had enough light that I was more afraid to stay than to go. Two weeks before we left, a check came in the mail that, after tithe, covered all of our domestic bills.

It was shouting ground for me. I had not seen the Lord help me in the other ministries that I had attempted to do, but now it was obvious He was helping me. Knowing and seeing that eased the stress like never before. My faith began to increase as I saw the Lord step in and take care of the details.

In that first trip, we had seven meetings, and one came open while we were out on the trip, so we did eight meetings in two and a half months, and drove clear around the United States of America. Out of those eight meetings only one pastor knew me. All of the others said, *"I don't know who you are, but I cannot get you off my mind, so I figured the Lord wanted me to have you in."* All of the meetings went very well, with all of the churches asking us to come back.

My first meeting of that first trip around the United States was a tent meeting. It was held on the grounds of the church. I preached, and each night people were stirred. When I was done preaching and it came time for the altar call, the altar was full of people crying, praying, and getting things right with the Lord. I forget the exact number, but there were people saved in the meeting also. It was great!

I was finally in God's perfect will for my life, and it felt so good. For the next year or so, when I would write my prayer letter, or in my conversation to Terri, I would say, *"The Lord keeps confirming the call of Evangelism."*

She would look at me with exasperation as if to say, *"You mean you still have a doubt?"* Well it wasn't so much a doubt of His call, as it was that I just could not believe that I was an evangelist. But I was, and I am, and that is God's will for my life. From the trials and mistakes of the years, I can say that I have no doubt as to His will for my life.

Ah yes! God's will! That duty, that treasure, that privilege!